Rick Steves'
SNAPSHOT

Naples & the Amalfi Coast

CONTENTS

INTRODUCTION

This Snapshot guide, excerpted from my guidebook *Rick Steves' Italy*, introduces you to Naples, Pompeii, and the Amalfi Coast. The gritty, historic port city of Naples is arguably Italy's wildest urban jungle, with a uniquely vibrant street life. Enjoy a pizza in its birthplace, and explore the city's excellent Archaeological Museum. Then head into the countryside to unearth ancient history at Pompeii and Herculaneum, well-preserved Roman towns in the shadow of the steaming Mt. Vesuvius.

An hour to the south, Sorrento kicks off the gloriously scenic Amalfi Coast, where buses filled with white-knuckle tourists take turns squeezing along an impossibly narrow sea-view road. Relax in stylish Sorrento, hilly Positano, or low-key Amalfi, and side-trip to the ancient Greek temples at Paestum, or to the jet-set isle of Capri, with its otherworldly Blue Grotto.

To help you have the best trip possible, I've included the following topics in this book:

• **Planning Your Time,** with advice on how to make the most of your limited time

• **Orientation,** including tourist information (abbreviated as TI), tips on public transportation, local tour options, and helpful hints

• **Sights** with ratings:

▲▲▲—Don't miss

▲▲—Try hard to see

▲—Worthwhile if you can make it

No rating—Worth knowing about

• **Sleeping** and **Eating,** with good-value recommendations in every price range

• **Connections,** with tips on trains, buses, and driving

Practicalities, near the end of this book, has information on money, phoning, hotel reservations, transportation, and more, plus Italian survival phrases.

To travel smartly, read this little book in its entirety before you go. It's my hope that this guide will make your trip more meaningful and rewarding. Traveling like a temporary local, you'll get the absolute most out of every mile, minute, and dollar.

Buon viaggio!

Rick Steves

NAPLES

Napoli

If you like Italy as far south as Rome, go farther south—it gets better. If Italy is getting on your nerves, don't go farther. Italy intensifies as you plunge deeper. Naples is Italy in the extreme—its best (birthplace of pizza and Sophia Loren) and its worst (home of the Camorra, Naples' "family" of organized crime).

Neapolis ("new city") was a thriving Greek commercial center 2,500 years ago. Today, it remains southern Italy's leading city. Naples impresses visitors with one of Europe's top archaeological museums (with the artistic treasures of Pompeii), fascinating churches that convey the city's unique personality and powerful devotion, an underground warren of Greek and Roman ruins, fine works of art (including pieces by Caravaggio, who lived here for a time), and evocative nativity scenes (called *presepi*). Naples, of course, makes the best pizza you'll find anywhere, and tasty pastries as well (try the crispy, ricotta-stuffed *sfogliatella*). But more than anything, Naples has a brash and vibrant street life—"Italy in your face" in ways both good and bad. Walking through its colorful old town is one of my favorite experiences anywhere in Europe. For a grand overlook,

head to the hilltop viewpoint (San Martino) for sweeping views of the city and its bay.

Naples—Italy's third-largest city, with more than one million people—has almost no open spaces or parks, which makes its position as Europe's most densely populated city plenty evident. Watching the police try to enforce traffic sanity is almost comical in Italy's grittiest, most polluted, and most crime-ridden city. But Naples surprises the observant traveler with its impressive knack for living, eating, and raising children in the streets with good humor and decency. Overcome your fear of being run down or ripped off long enough to talk with people. Enjoy a few smiles and jokes with the man running the neighborhood tripe shop, or the woman taking her day-care class on a walk through the traffic.

The pulse of Italy throbs in Naples. Like Cairo or Mumbai, it's appalling and captivating at the same time, the closest thing to "reality travel" that you'll find in Western Europe. But this tangled mess still somehow manages to breathe, laugh, and sing—with a joyful Italian accent. Thanks to its reputation as a crime-ridden and dangerous place, Naples doesn't get nearly as many tourists as it deserves. While Naples has its problems, it has improved a lot in recent years. And even though it's a bit edgy, I feel comfortable here. Naples richly rewards those who venture in.

Naples is also the springboard for a full region of sightseeing treats (covered in the next three chapters): Just beyond Naples are the remarkable ruins of Pompeii and Herculaneum, and the brooding volcano that did them both in, Mount Vesuvius. A few more miles down the road is the pleasant resort town of Sorrento and the offshore escape isle of Capri. And plunging even farther south, you'll reach the dramatic scenery of the Amalfi Coast.

Planning Your Time

Naples makes an ideal day trip either from Rome or from the comfortable home base of Sorrento, located an hour south. Or stow your bag at the station and see Naples in a few hours while you change trains here on the way between Rome and Sorrento. A little Naples goes a long way; if you're not comfortable in chaotic and congested cities, think twice before spending the night here. But those who are intrigued by the city's sights and street life enjoy overnighting in Naples.

On a quick visit, start with the Archaeological Museum (closed Tue), follow my "A Slice of Neapolitan Life" self-guided walk, and celebrate your survival with pizza. With more time, dip into more churches, go underground to see Greek and Roman ruins, and consider ascending San Martino for the view. Of course, Naples is huge. But even with limited time, if you stick to the prescribed route and grab a cab when you're lost or tired, it's fun. Treat yourself well in Naples; the city is cheap by Italian standards. This is a place where splurging on a sane and comfortable hotel is a particularly worthwhile investment.

For a blitz tour from Rome, you could have breakfast on an early Rome-Naples express train (for example, Mon-Fri 7:35-8:45), do Naples and Pompeii in a day, and be back in Rome in time for bed. That's exhausting, but more memorable than a fourth day in Rome.

Remember that on summer afternoons, Naples' street life slows and many churches and museums close as the temperature soars. The city comes back to life in the early evening.

Orientation to Naples

Naples is set deep inside the large and curving Bay of Naples, with Mount Vesuvius looming just five miles away. Although Naples is a sprawling city, its fairly compact core contains the most interesting sights. The tourist's Naples is a triangle, with its points at the Centrale train station in the east, the Archaeological Museum to the west, and the Piazza del Plebiscito (with the Royal Palace) and the port to the south. Steep hills rise above this historic core, including San Martino, capped with a mighty fortress.

Tourist Information

Central Naples has six TIs (run variously by the city, the region, and a local business association), all of which are equally incapable of dispensing reliable advice. All are understaffed and have little to offer besides free maps. The most convenient—but perhaps least helpful—is in the **Centrale train station** (daily 9:00-18:00, near track 23, operated by a private agency, tel. 081-268-779). This is a convenient place to buy Campania ArteCard passes (see sidebar).

Other TIs are scattered around town: There are two near **Piazza del Plebiscito,** near the port: one right on the piazza at #14, under the arches to the right of church entrance (Mon-Fri 9:00-19:00, closed Sat-Sun, tel. 081-795-6162); and another by the entrance to the Galleria Umberto I shopping mall, across from Teatro di San Carlo (Mon-Sat 9:00-19:00, Sun 9:00-14:00, tel. 081-402-394). Along Spaccanapoli, there's an office across from the **Church of Gesù Nuovo** (Mon-Sat 9:00-19:00, Sun 9:00-14:00, tel. 081-551-2701). By the Museo Metro stop, in the park next to the **Archaeological Museum,** is a tiny information kiosk (Mon-Fri 10:00-17:00, Sat 10:00-14:00, closed Sun). And cruise-ship passengers exiting the **cruise terminal** complex pass through a little checkpoint (marked *Molo Angioino*) that has a small TI.

For information online, the best overall website is www.in-aples.it. At www.inaples.it/eng/quinapoli.htm, you can download their big (100-plus-page, 50 MB) PDF version of the *Qui Napoli* booklet, which lists museum hours, events, and transportation info. (Due to funding cuts, the booklet is no longer distributed in paper form.)

Naples

To Museo di Capodimonte   *Cavour*
Piazza Cavour
VIA FORIA   CARBONARA
Piazza Capuana
CASANOVA
Airport Bus
VIA DUOMO
S. APOST.
POERIO
FIRENZE

ARCHAEO-LOGICAL MUSEUM
Museo
S. PAOLO
DUOMO
PIO MONTE MISERICORDIA
VIA TRIBUNALI
#1 *Piazza Garibaldi*
FISH MKT.
CENTRALE STN.(F.S.)

Montesanto Metro & Funicular
Piazza Dante
Dante
CAPPELLA SANSEVERO
SAN DOM.
VIA S. BIAGIO
FORCELLA
Porta Nolana
To Pompeii (Ruins) & Sorrento

TARSIA
SCURA
VIA P.
GESÙ NUOVO
VIA B. CROCE
SPACCANAPOLI
UMBERTO I
PORTA NOLANA CIRCUMVESUVIANA TERMINUS STN.

SANTA CHIARA & CLOISTER
CORSO
NUOVA MARINA

VIA PIGNASECCA
VIA F. EMAN.
VIA MORGANTINA
Piazza Carità
Piazza Bovio
Università
VIA DIAZ
VIA ROMA
Toledo
DEPRETIS
VIA C. COLOMBO

SPANISH QUARTER
CORSO VIT. EMAN.
VIA TOLEDO
Municipio
Bus to Airport
GALLERIA UMBERTO I
Piazza Municipio
Tram to Train Station
Port

Centrale Funicular
TEATRO DI SANCARLO
CASTEL NUOVO
STAZIONE MARITTIMA
Car Ferries to Sicily & Sardinia

To ❸
Piazza del Plebiscito
ROYAL PALACE
MOLO BEVERELLO DOCK

S. FRAN. DI PAOLA
See "Slice of Neapolitan Life Walk" detail map
To Sorrento, Capri, Ischia & Procida

VITTORIO TUNNEL
VIA NAZARIO SAURO
Bay of Naples

VIA PARTENOPE
To Lungomare
❹

CASTEL DELL'OVO
BORGO MARINARO
500 Meters
500 Yards

❶ Grand Hotel Europa
❷ Hotel Potenza, La Cantina dei Mille & Iris Ristorante
❸ To Pinto-Storey Hotel
❹ Ristorante la Scialuppa

Arrival in Naples

By Train

There are several Naples train stations, but all trains coming into town stop at either Napoli Centrale or Garibaldi—which are essentially the same place, with Centrale on top of Garibaldi. Stretching in front of this station complex is the vast and gritty Piazza Garibaldi.

Centrale is the main station, serving trains on the main line. It's been spruced up in the last few years and has lots of facilities, including a small TI (near track 23), an ATM (at Banco di Napoli

Planning Your Time in the Region

On a quick trip, give the entire area—including Sorrento and Naples—a minimum of three days. If you use Sorrento as your sunny springboard (see Sorrento chapter), spend a day in Naples, a day exploring the Amalfi Coast, and a day split between Pompeii and the town of Sorrento. While Paestum (Greek temples), Mount Vesuvius, Herculaneum (an ancient Roman site like Pompeii), and the island of Capri are decent destinations, they are worthwhile only if you have more time. For a map, see page 5.

The **Campania ArteCard** regional pass may save you a few euros if you're here for two or three days, using public transportation, and plan to visit at least two of the region's three big sights: Pompeii (€11), Herculaneum (€11), and Naples' Archaeological Museum (€8). There are several Campania ArteCard versions, covering varying combinations of sights and public transportation. The three-day, €32 Tutta la Regione version is especially good if you'll be visiting both Naples and Sorrento; it includes free entry to two sights (plus a decent discount off others) and transportation within Naples, on the Circumvesuviana train, and on Amalfi Coast buses. The three-day, €30 Archeologia del Golfo version makes sense if you base yourself in Naples; it covers all three of the main archaeological sites plus several minor ones and transportation as far out as Pompeii. Cards are sold at some Naples TIs and at participating sights (cards activate on first use, expire 3 days later at midnight, www.campaniartecard.it).

near track 24), a baggage check (€5/5 hours, then €0.70/hour, daily 8:00-20:00, marked *deposito bagagli*, near track 5), and a ticket office (daily 5:50-21:10).

Garibaldi is a commuter rail station on the lower level of the Centrale Station complex. Get off here if arriving on the Circumvesuviana train line from Sorrento or Pompeii (the line terminates one stop deeper into downtown, at the Napoli Porta Nolana station). Garibaldi is also used by a few regular trains to make a quick stop as they barrel through. For more on the Circumvesuviana, see "Getting Around the Region," later.

By Ferry or Cruise Ship

Naples is a ferry hub with great boat connections to Sorrento, Capri, and other nearby destinations. Ferries use the Molo Beverello dock, while cruise ships use the nearby Stazione Marittima cruise terminal. The two docks are side-by-side at the port on the southeast edge of downtown Naples, near Castel Nuovo and the grand square called Piazza del Plebiscito. In the covered area between the cruise-terminal buildings, you'll find cafés and various shops, including a tobacco shop (where you can buy bus tickets).

Out by the street is the recommended Ontano Tours travel agency (see "Helpful Hints," later).

Whether arriving by ferry or cruise ship, you can get to the city center by taxi, bus, or on foot; the Alibus shuttle bus runs to the airport (see "By Plane," next; the stop is a couple of blocks inland from the port, between Castel Nuovo and Teatro di San Carlo).

The **taxi** stand is in front of the port area; figure €12-15 to get to the train station or to the Archaeological Museum.

Tram #1 stops at the busy road directly in front of the cruise terminal and heads to Piazza Garibaldi and the train station, where you can connect to trains to sights outside of town (6/hour, 15 minutes, buy €1.20 ticket at tobacco shop, validate ticket in yellow box on the bus as you board); to reach the Circumvesuviana commuter line to Pompeii or Sorrento, you can hop off this tram a bit earlier, at Porta Nolana, to catch the train at its starting point.

Straight ahead across the road from the cruise terminal (on the right side of the big fortress) is a drab square called Piazza Municipio; from here, a **bus** stop to Naples' Archaeological Museum is a half-block down on Via Agostino Depretis (#R4, departs every 10-15 minutes, ride six stops to Piazza Museo). The new Municipio **Metro** stop, which may open here in 2014, will zip you to the museum faster (take line 1 three stops, to Museo).

On foot, it's a seven-minute **walk**—past the gigantic Castel Nuovo—to Piazza del Plebiscito and the old city center: After crossing the busy street in front of the port, head up the ramp just to the right of the castle. At the top, angle left, past Teatro di San Carlo, to Piazza del Plebiscito. From this square, you could do a truncated version of my self-guided walk (begin near the end of "Part 2," do that stretch backwards up the hill, then launch right into "Part 3").

By Plane

Naples International Airport (a.k.a. Capodichino, code: NAP) is located a few miles outside of town (tel. 081-789-6111 for operator, tel. 848-888-777 for info, www.gesac.it). Alibus shuttle buses zip you from the airport to Naples' Centrale train station/Piazza Garibaldi in 15 minutes, and then head to the port/Piazza Municipio for boats to Capri and Sorrento (buses run daily 6:30-24:00, 3/hour, less frequent early and late, 30 minutes to the port, €3, turn right as you exit and find platform #2 at the bus stop, pay driver, stops at train station and port only). It's tough to get a cabbie to use the meter from the airport, but a taxi ride should cost about €20.

To reach **Sorrento** from Naples Airport, take the direct Curreri bus (daily at 9:00, 11:00, 13:00, 14:30, 16:30, and 19:30; 1.25 hours, €10, pay driver, tel. 081-801-5420, www.curreriviaggi.it).

NAPLES

Helpful Hints

Theft Alert: While most travelers visit Naples completely safely, err on the side of caution. Don't venture into neighborhoods that make you uncomfortable. The areas close to the train station are especially seedy. Walk with confidence, as if you know where you're going and what you're doing. Touristy Spaccanapoli and the posh Via Toledo shopping boulevard are more upscale, but you'll still see rowdy kids and panhandlers. Assume able-bodied beggars are thieves.

Stick to busy streets and beware of gangs of hoodlums. A third of the city is unemployed, and past local governments have set an example that the Mafia would be proud of. Assume con artists are more clever than you. Any jostle or commotion is probably a thief-team smokescreen. To keep bags safe, it's probably best to leave them at your hotel or at the left-luggage office in Centrale Station.

Always walk on the sidewalk (even if the locals don't) and carry your bag on the side away from the street—thieves on scooters have been known to snatch bags as they swoop by. The less you have dangling from you (including cameras and necklaces), the better.

Perhaps your biggest risk of theft is while catching or riding the Circumvesuviana commuter train. If you're connecting from a long-distance express, you'll be stepping from a relatively secure compartment into an often crowded and dingy train, where disoriented tourists with luggage delicately mix with the residents of Naples' most down-at-heel districts. It's prime hunting ground for thieves. While I ride the Circumvesuviana comfortably and safely, each year I hear of many travelers who get ripped off on this ride. You won't be mugged—but you may be conned or pickpocketed. Especially late at night, the Circumvesuviana train is plagued by intimidating ruffians. For maximum safety and peace of mind, sit in the front car, where the driver will double as your protector, and avoid riding it after dark.

Con artists may say you need to "transfer" by taxi to catch the Circumvesuviana; you don't. Carry your own bags and keep valuables buttoned up.

Traffic Safety: In Naples, red lights are discretionary, and pedestrians need to be wary, particularly of motor scooters. Even on "pedestrian" streets, stay alert to avoid being sideswiped by scooters that nudge their way through the crowds. Keep children close. Smart tourists jaywalk in the shadow of bold and confident locals, who generally ignore crosswalks. Wait for a break in traffic, cross with confidence, and make eye contact with approaching drivers. The traffic will stop.

Supermarket: Superò is a block off Piazza Dante, close to my recommended hotels along Via Toledo and Spaccanapoli (Mon-Sat 8:30-20:30, Sun 8:30-14:00, Via San Domenico Soriano 20e).

Laundry: Laundry DIY, between Piazza Dante and the Archaeological Museum, will—despite their name—do your laundry for you (€8/load, Mon-Fri 8:00-19:30, Sat 8:00-13:15, closed Sun, Via Vincenzo Bellini 50, mobile 339-318-0876).

Getting Around Naples

Naples' entire public transportation system—Metro, buses, funicular railways, and the single tram line—uses the same tickets, which must be stamped as you enter (in the yellow machines). A €1.30 single transit ticket gives you the run of the system for 1.5 hours, with unlimited changes. Tickets are sold at *tabacchi* stores and (sometimes) at station windows; the few ticket machines you'll see are usually out of order. A *giornaliero* day pass costs €3.70 (€3.10 on weekends) and pays for itself with three rides, but can be hard to find; most *tabacchi* stores don't sell them. Many versions of the Campania ArteCard include free public transport in Naples, but the card doesn't work in the subway and funicular turnstiles; you'll have to show it to the staff, who will open the gate for you. For general information, maps, and fares in English, visit www.unicocampania.it. For schedules, your only option is the Italian-only site www.anm.it.

By Subway: Naples' subway, the Metropolitana, has three main lines. Line 1 is currently being extended, adding several new stations that will make it very useful for tourists. Unless otherwise noted, the following stops are open (completion dates for the rest are subject to change): From the Museo stop (Archaeological Museum), line 1 heads to Dante (at Piazza Dante, between the museum and Spaccanapoli), Toledo (south end of Via Toledo, near Piazza del Plebiscito), Municipio (likely to open by 2014; at Piazza Municipio, just above the harbor and cruise terminal), Università (the university), Duomo (likely to open in 2015; near the cathedral and the end of my self-guided walk), and Garibaldi (likely open by late 2013; on Piazza Garibaldi in front of Centrale Station).

Line 2 (technically part of the Italian rail system) is most useful for getting from the train station to the Archaeological Museum quickly: It runs from Centrale Station (catch it downstairs—the stop is called Garibaldi) to Piazza Cavour (by the Archaeological Museum). Other stops on line 2 include Montesanto (top of Spanish Quarter and Spaccanapoli street, and base of funicular up to San Martino), and Amedeo (recommended hotel in the Chiaia district). The new line 6 is not yet complete; it will begin at Municipio and head west—unlikely to be of much use to tourists.

NAPLES

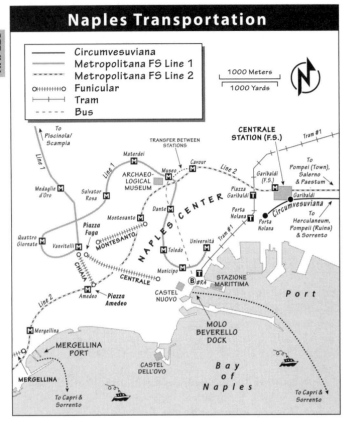

Naples Transportation

— Circumvesuviana
— Metropolitana FS Line 1
---- Metropolitana FS Line 2
o+++++++o Funicular
⊢—•—•—⊣ Tram
----- Bus

1000 Meters
1000 Yards

By Funicular: Central Naples' three funiculars *(funicolare)* carry commuters and sightseers into the hilly San Martino neighborhood just west of downtown. All three converge near Piazza Fuga, a short walk from the hilltop fortress and monastery/museum. The Centrale line runs from the Spanish Quarter, just near Piazza del Plebiscito and the Toledo Metro stop; the Montesanto line from the Montesanto Metro stop and Via Pignasecca market zone; and the Chiaia line from near the Piazza Amadeo Metro stop.

By Bus: Buses can be handy for certain trips, such as getting from the port to the Archaeological Museum (bus #R4), or if you need to curtail my self-guided walk from Via Toledo back to the station. But buses are crowded and poorly signed, and aren't a user-friendly option for uninitiated newcomers.

By Tram: The single tram line #1 runs along Corso Garibaldi (at the other end of the big square from Centrale Station) and down to the waterfront, terminating by the ferry and cruise terminals. It's useful if you're connecting from boat to train, or returning to the port after finishing my self-guided walk.

By Taxi: Taxi drivers in Naples are notorious for overcharging. A short ride in town should cost €10-12. Ask for the *tariffa predeterminata* (a fixed rate). Your hotel can tell you what a given ride should cost. There are some legitimate extra charges (baggage fees, €2.50 supplement after 22:00 or all day Sun and holidays).

Tours in Naples

Local Guides
Pina Esposito knows her ancient archaeology and art and does fine private walking and driving tours of Naples and the region (Pompeii, Capri, etc.), including Naples' Archaeological Museum (€60/hour, 2-hour minimum, 10 percent off with this book, lower rates for full-day tours, mobile 366-622-8217, giuseppina.esposito20@istruzione.it). The team at **Mondo Guide** also offers private tours of the museum (€120/2 hours), city (€240/4 hours), and region, along with a special deal for my readers—see next page (tel. 081-751-3290, www.mondoguide.it, info@mondoguide.it).

Hop-on, Hop-off Bus Tours
CitySightseeing Napoli tour buses make three different loops through the city, allowing riders to get on and off to explore. While the city's most engaging charms are buried in the tight tangle of lanes near Spaccanapoli, a bus tour does give you a better sense of the greater Naples that this chapter largely ignores (€22, tickets good for 24 hours, sparse frequency—4-11/day depending on route, buy from driver or from kiosk at Piazza Municipio in front of Castel Nuovo near the port, scant recorded narration; for details, see the brochure at hotels and TI, tel. 081-551-7279, www.napoli.city-sightseeing.it).

Cruise-Ship Excursions
Convenient for cruise-ship passengers, consider the **Can't Be Missed** tour company, which gives you a quick look at Naples, Sorrento, and Pompeii with a small group and local guide for €65 (meet at 8:30 in front of port, bus leaves at 9:00, returns at 17:00, Pompeii ticket extra, mobile 329-129-8182, www.cantbemissedtours.com).

Self-Guided Tour

▲▲▲Archaeological Museum (Museo Archeologico)
This museum offers the best possible peek at the art and decorations of Pompeii and Herculaneum, the two ancient burgs that were buried in ash by the eruption of Mount Vesuvius in A.D. 79. For lovers of antiquity, this museum alone makes Naples a worth-

Mondo's Tours of Pompeii, Naples, and the Amalfi Coast for My Readers

Mondo Tours, a big Naples-based company (listed on previous page), offers co-op tours for Rick Steves readers. The idea—new for 2014—is to allow you the luxury of having a private, professional guide at a fraction of the usual cost (because you'll be sharing the expense with other travelers using this book). If you're willing to be a guinea pig for this experiment, sign up on their website, www.mondoguide.it (look for the Rick Steves tab). As they continually update departures on their online schedule, check the website to see the latest. Add your name as a promise to be there, then pay the guide (cash only) at the start of the tour. Pre-registration is required, and each tour will depart only if at least eight people have signed up (16-person maximum). Check the website the day before to be sure your tour received enough sign-ups to actually run (you can contact Mondo Tours at: tel. 081-751-3290, mobile 340-460-5254, info@mondoguide.it).

As this is a new system, please send your feedback—good or bad—to books@ricksteves.com. If you can't find the Rick Steves tab on Mondo's site, it means that the tours are no longer offered.

This program, which runs only from April through October of 2014, covers the tours in this region where travelers will get the most value out of this service.

Pompeii Tour: This two-hour guided walk brings to life the ruins of the excavated city (€12, doesn't include €11 Pompeii entry but guide will collect money and buy tickets, likely Mon-Fri at 10:30 but confirm schedule online; meet at Ristorante Suisse on Piazza Esedra (a 5-minute walk from the train station—exiting the

while stop. When Pompeii was excavated in the late 1700s, Naples' Bourbon king bellowed, "Bring me the best of what you find!" The finest art and artifacts ended up here, and today, the ancient sites themselves are impressive but barren. (If you'd like to visit those sites—both an easy train ride from Naples—see the next chapter.)

Cost and Hours: €8, sometimes more for temporary exhibits, Wed-Mon 9:00-19:30, closed Tue, last entry 30 minutes before closing. Early and temporary closures are noted on a board near the ticket office.

Getting There: To take the **subway** from Centrale Station, follow signs to the Metro, called *Metropolitana*, located downstairs at the Garibaldi subway station (across from track 13). Buy a single transit ticket at the newsstand or a tobacco shop (unless you're station, turn right, pass the Porta Marina entrance, and continue down the hill to the restaurant, on the right).

Historic Naples Walk: Naples is a challenge to enjoy and understand; on this three-hour walk, a local Neapolitan guide helps you uncover the true character of the city (€20; likely Mon, Wed, and Fri at 15:00 but confirm schedule online). Tours meet at the steps of the National Museum of Archaeology (which is not included in the walk) in hopes that you can do the museum on your own before joining your guide.

Pompeii and Naples Combo: Combine the two tours listed above for €30 (only possible Mon, Wed, and Fri; you'll need to connect the two tours on your own; ideally, head straight from Pompeii to Naples in time to briefly tour the highlights of the National Museum of Archaeology before the Historic Naples Walk starts).

Full-Day Amalfi Coast Minibus Tour from Sorrento: The Amalfi Coast can be complicated and time-consuming to visit on your own, making a shared minibus the simplest and most affordable way to enjoy the sights. This nine-hour trip will save time and money and maximize your experience. It begins in Sorrento and heads south for the breathtaking drive (lightly narrated by your driver), photo stops, and an hour or two on your own in each of the three main towns—Positano, Amalfi, and Ravello—before returning to Sorrento (€45, likely Mon-Fri at 9:00 but confirm schedule online, meet overlooking the gorge in front of Hotel Antiche Mura, at Via Fuorimura 7, a block inland from Piazza Tasso).

getting a pass), and validate it in the small yellow boxes near the escalator going down to the tracks. You're looking for trains heading in the direction of Pozzuoli (generally depart from track 4). Hop on any train that comes through (confirm by its sign or with a local that it's going to Pozzuoli), and ride the subway one stop to Cavour. As you leave the Metro, exit and hike five minutes uphill through the park along the busy street. Look for a grand old red building located up a flight of stairs at the top of the block.

If taking the Metro back to Centrale Station, make sure to catch your train in the Cavour subway station, rather than at the connected Museo stop (which is on a different line).

Figure on €12 for a **taxi** from the train station to the museum.

Information: The shop sells a worthwhile *National Archaeological Museum of Naples* guidebook for €12. Tel. 081-442-2149.

Tours: My self-guided tour (below) covers all the basics. For more detail, the decent **audioguide** costs €5 (at ticket desk). If you want a **guided tour,** book Pina Esposito (see "Tours in Naples," earlier).

NAPLES

Baggage Check: Bag check is obligatory and free.

Photography: Photos are allowed without a flash.

Eating: The museum has no café, but vending machines sell drinks and snacks at reasonable prices. There are several good places to grab a meal within a few blocks.

Self-Guided Tour: Overview

Entering the museum, stand at the base of the grand staircase. To your right, on the ground floor, are the larger-than-life statues of

the Farnese Collection, starring the *Toro Farnese* and the *Farnese Hercules*. Up the stairs on the mezzanine level (turn left at the lion) are mosaics and frescoes from Pompeii, including the *Battle of Alexander* and the Secret Room of erotic art. On the top floor are more frescoes, a scale model of Pompeii, and bronze statues from Herculaneum. WCs are behind the staircase.

• *From the base of the grand staircase, turn right through the door marked* Collezione Farnese *and head to the far end—walking through a rich collection of idealistic and realistic ancient portrait busts—to reach the farthest room (Sala XIII).*

Ground Floor: The Farnese Collection

The museum's ground floor alone has enough Greek and Roman art to put any museum on the map. This floor has nothing from Pompeii; its highlight is the Farnese Collection, a grand hall of huge, bright, and wonderfully restored statues excavated from Rome's Baths of Caracalla. Peruse the larger-than-life statues filling the hall. They were dug up in the 1540s at the behest of Alessandro Farnese (by then Pope Paul III) while he was building the family palace on the Campo dei Fiori in Rome. His main purpose in excavating the baths was to scavenge quality building stone. The sculptures were a nice extra and helped the palace come in under budget on decorations. In the 1700s, the collection ended up in the hands of Charles, the Bourbon king of Naples (whose mother was a Farnese). His son, the next king, had it brought to Naples.

• *Quick—look down to the left end of the hall. There's a woman being tied to a snorting bull.*

The tangled *Toro Farnese* tells a thrilling Greek myth. At 13 feet, it's the tallest ancient marble group ever found, and the largest intact statue from antiquity. A third-century A.D. copy of a lost bronze Hellenistic original, it was carved out of one piece of marble. Michelangelo and others "restored" it at the pope's request—meaning that they integrated surviving bits into a new work. Panels on the wall show which pieces were actually carved by Michelangelo (in blue on the chart): the head of the woman in back, the torso of the aunt under the bull, and the dog. (Imagine how the statue would stand out if it were thoughtfully lit and not surrounded by white walls.)

Here's the tragic story behind the statue: Once upon an ancient Greek time, King Lycus was bewitched by Dirce. He abandoned his pregnant wife, Antiope (standing regally in the background). The single mom gave birth to twin boys (shown here). When they grew up, they killed their deadbeat dad and tied Dirce to the horns of a bull to be bashed against a mountain. Captured in marble, the action is thrilling: cape flailing, dog snarling, hooves in the air. You can almost hear the bull snorting. And in the back, Antiope oversees this harsh ancient justice with satisfaction.

At the opposite end of the hall stands the *Farnese Hercules*. The great Greek hero is exhausted. He leans wearily on his club (draped with his lion skin) and bows his head. He's just finished the daunting Eleventh Labor, having traveled the world, fought men and gods, freed Prometheus from his rock, and carried Atlas' weight of the world on his shoulders. Now he's returned with the prize: the golden apples of the gods, which he cups behind his back. But, after all that, he's just been told he has to return the apples and do one final labor: descend into Hell itself. Oh, man.

The 10-foot colossus is a third-century A.D. Roman marble copy (signed by "Glykon") of a fourth-century B.C. Greek bronze original (probably by Lysippos). The statue was enormously famous in its day. Dozens of copies—some marble, some bronze—have been found in Roman villas and baths. This version was unearthed in Rome's Baths of Caracalla in 1546, along with the *Toro Farnese*.

The *Farnese Hercules* was equally famous in the 16th-18th centuries. Tourists flocked to Rome to admire it, art students studied it from afar in prints, Louis XIV made a copy for Versailles, and petty nobles everywhere put small-scale knock-offs in their gardens. This curly-haired version of Hercules became the modern world's image of the Greek hero.

• *Backtrack to the main entry hall, then head up to the mezzanine level (turning left at the lion).*

Mezzanine: Pompeiian Mosaics and the Secret Room

Most of these mosaics—of animals, musicians, and geometric designs—were taken from Pompeii's House of the Faun. Walk into the third room and look for the 20-inch-high statue in a freestanding glass case: the house's delightful centerpiece, the *Dancing Faun.* This rare surviving Greek bronze statue (from the fourth century B.C.) is surrounded by some of the best mosaics of that age.

A museum highlight, just beyond the statue, is the grand *Battle of Alexander,* a second-century B.C. copy of the original Greek fresco, done a century earlier. It decorated a floor in the House of the Faun and was found intact; the damage you see occurred as this treasure was moved from Pompeii to the king's collection here. Alexander (left side of the scene, with curly hair and sideburns) is about to defeat the Persians under Darius (central figure, in chariot with turban and beard). This pivotal victory allowed Alexander to quickly overrun much of Asia (331 B.C.). Alexander is the only one without a helmet...a confident master of the battlefield while everyone else is fighting for their lives, eyes bulging with fear. Notice how the horses, already in retreat, add to the scene's propaganda value. Notice also the shading and perspective,

which Renaissance artists would later work so hard to accomplish. (A modern reproduction of the mosaic is now back in Pompeii, at the House of the Faun.)

Farther on, the **Secret Room** *(Gabinetto Segreto)* contains a sizable assortment of erotic frescoes, well-hung pottery, and perky statues that once decorated bedrooms, meeting rooms, brothels, and even shops at Pompeii and Herculaneum. These bawdy statues and frescoes—many of them once displayed in Pompeii's grandest houses—were entertainment for guests. (By the time they made it to this museum, in 1819, the frescoes could be viewed only with permission from the king—see the letters in the glass case just outside the door.) The Roman nobles commissioned the wildest scenes imaginable. Think of them as ancient dirty jokes.

At the entrance, you're enthusiastically greeted by big stone penises that once projected over Pompeii's doorways. A massive phallus was not necessarily a sexual symbol, but a magical amulet used against the "evil eye." It symbolized fertility, happiness, good luck, riches, straight A's, and general well-being.

Circulating counterclockwise through this section, look for the following: a faun playfully pulling the sheet off a beautiful woman, only to be grossed out by a hermaphrodite's plumbing (perhaps the original *"Mamma mia!"*; #12); horny pygmies from Africa in action (#27); a toga with an embarrassing bulge (#34); a particularly high-quality statue of a goat and a satyr illustrating an act of sodomy (#36); and, watching over it all with remarkable aplomb, Venus, the patron goddess of Pompeii (#39).

The back room is furnished and decorated the way an ancient brothel might have been. The 10 frescoes on the wall functioned as both a menu of services offered and as a kind of *Kama Sutra* of sex positions. The glass cases contain more phallic art.

• *So, now that your travel buddy is finally showing a little interest in art...finish up your visit by climbing the stairs to the top floor.*

Top Floor: Frescoes, Statues, Artifacts, and a Model of Pompeii

At the top of the stairs, go through the center door to enter a grand, empty hall. This was the **great hall** of the university (17th and 18th centuries) until the building became the royal museum in 1777. Walk to the center. The sundial (from 1791) still works. Look up to the far-right corner of the hall and find the tiny pinhole. At noon (13:00 in summer), a ray of sun enters the hall and strikes the sundial, showing the time of the year...if you know your zodiac.

To your left, you'll see a door marked *affreschi*. This leads to eight rooms showing off the museum's impressive and well-described collection of (non-erotic) **frescoes** taken from the walls of Pompeii villas. Pompeiians loved to decorate their homes with scenes from mythology (Hercules' labors, Venus and Mars in love), landscapes, everyday market scenes, and faux architecture. Continue around this wing counterclockwise (with the courtyard on your left) through rooms of artifacts found at Pompeii. At the far end is a scale model of Pompeii as excavated in 1879 *(plastic di Pompeii)*. Another model (on the wall) shows the site in 2004, after more excavations.

NAPLES

• *Eventually you'll end up back in the great hall.*

Step out to the top landing of the staircase you climbed earlier. Turn left and go down, then up, 16 steps and into the wing labeled *La Villa dei Papiri.* This ex-hibition shows off artifacts (particularly bronze statues) from the Herculaneum hol-iday home of Julius Caesar's father-in-law. In the second room (numbered CXVI), look into the lifelike blue eyes of the intense *Cor-*

ridore (athletes), bent on doing their best. The *Five Dancers,* with their inlaid-ivory eyes and graceful poses, decorated a portico. The next room (CXVII) has more fine works: *Resting Hermes* (with his tired little heel wings) is taking a break. Nearby, the *Drunken Faun* (singing and snapping his fingers to the beat, a wineskin at his side) is clearly living for today—true to the *carpe diem* preaching of the Epicurean philosophy. Caesar's father-in-law was a fan of Epicurean philosophy, and his library—containing 2,000 papyrus scrolls—supported his outlook. Back by the entrance, check out the plans of the villa, and in the side room, see how the half-burned scrolls were unrolled and (with luck) read after excavation in the 1750s.

• *Return to the ground floor. The exit hall (right) leads around the museum courtyard and to the gift shop.*

Doriforo

For extra credit on your way out, find **Dori-foro.** He was last spotted on the right as you walk down the exit hall. (If he's been moved, ask a guard, *"Dov'è il Doriforo?"*) This seven-foot-tall "spear-carrier" (the literal translation of *doriforo*) just stands there, as if holding a spear. What's the big deal about this statue, which looks like so many others? It's a mar-ble replica made by the Romans of one of the most-copied statues of antiquity, a fifth-cen-tury B.C. bronze Greek original by Polyclitus. This copy once stood in a Pompeii gym, where it inspired ancient athletes by showing the ideal proportions of Greek beauty. So full of motion, and so realistic in its *contrapposto* pose (weight on one foot), the *Doriforo* would later inspire Donatello and Michelangelo, helping to trigger the Renaissance. And so the glories of ancient Pompeii, once buried and forgotten, live on today.

Self-Guided Walk

▲▲▲A Slice of Neapolitan Life

This walk takes you from the Archaeological Museum through the heart of town and back to Centrale Station. Allow at least three hours, plus time for pizza and sightseeing stops. If you're in a rush, do it in half the time by walking briskly and skipping Part 2.

Naples, a living medieval city, is its own best sight. Couples artfully make love on Vespas surrounded by more fights and smiles per cobblestone than anywhere else in Italy. Rather than seeing Naples as a list of sights, visit its one great museum and then capture its essence by taking this walk through the core of the city.

Part 1: From the Archaeological Museum to Piazza Bellini and Piazza Dante

The first two parts of this walk are a mostly straight one-mile ramble down a fine boulevard (with a few colorful detours) to the waterfront at Piazza del Plebiscito. Your starting point is the Archaeological Museum (at the top of Piazza Cavour, Metro: Cavour or Museo; for a self-guided tour of the museum, see earlier). As you stroll, remember that here in Naples, red traffic lights are considered "decorations." When crossing a street, try to tag along with a native.
• *From the door of the Archaeological Museum, cross the street, veer right, and pass through the fancy mall.*

Galleria Principe di Napoli: This was named for the first male child of the royal Savoy family, the Prince of Naples. Walk directly through it, enjoying this fine shopping gallery from the late 19th century, similar to those popular in Paris and London. This is "Liberty Style," a variation of Art Nouveau (named for a British department store) that was in vogue at a time when Naples was nicknamed the "Paris of the South." Parisian artist Edgar Degas left Paris to adopt Naples—which he actually considered more cosmopolitan and sophisticated—as his hometown.
• *Leaving the gallery through the opposite end, walk one block downhill. At the fine Bellini Theater (in the Liberty Style), jog left one block, then turn right on Via Constantinopoli, continuing directly downhill to Piazza Bellini. As you walk, look up to enjoy architecture built in the late 19th century, when Naples was the last stop on Romantic Age travelers' Grand Tour of Europe. (From a tourism perspective, Sorrento only rose with the cultural and economic fall of Naples in the decades following Italian independence, around the early 20th century.)*

Soon you'll run into the ragtag urban park called...

NAPLES

"A Slice of Neapolitan Life" Walk

NAPLES

Piazza Bellini: Walking between columns of two grand churches, suddenly you're in neighborhood Napoli. A statue of Vincenzo Bellini marks the center of Piazza Bellini. It's dedicated to the Sicilian opera composer who worked here in the early 1800s. Survey the many balconies—and the people who use them as a "backyard" in this densely packed city. The apartment flats were originally palaces of noble families, as indicated by the stately family crests above grand doorways. Look down below the square to see the ruined Greek walls: tuff blocks without mortar. This was the wall, and you're standing on land that was outside of the town. You can see the street level from the fifth century B.C., when Neapolis—literally, "the new city"—was founded. For 2,500 years, laundry has blown in the breeze right here.

• *Walk 30 yards downhill. Stop at the horseshoe-shaped Port'Alba gate (on the right). Spin slowly 360 degrees and take in the scene. The proud tile across the street shows Piazza Bellini circa 1890. Learn to ignore graffiti (as the locals do). Pass through the gate, and stroll past the book stalls down Via Port'Alba to the next big square...*

Piazza Dante: This square is marked by a statue of Dante, the medieval poet. Fittingly, half the square is devoted to bookstores. Old Dante looks out over an urban area that was once grand, then chaotic, and is now slowly becoming grand again.

While this square feels perfectly Italian to me, for many Neapolitans it represents the repression of the central Italian state. When Napoleon was defeated, Naples briefly became its own independent kingdom. But within a few decades of Italian unification, in 1861, Naples went from being a thriving cultural and political capital to a provincial town, its money used to help establish the industrial strength of the north, its dialect considered backward, and its bureaucrats transferred to Rome.

Originally, a statue of a Spanish Bourbon king stood in the square. (The grand red-and-gray building is typical of Bourbon structures from that period.) But with the unification of Italy, the king, symbolic of Naples' colonial subjugation, was replaced by Dante, the father of the unified Italian language—a strong symbol of nationalism (and yet another form of subjugation).

The Neapolitan people are survivors. A long history of corrupt and greedy colonial overlords (German, Norman, French, Austrian, and Spanish) has taught Neapolitans to deal creatively with authority. Many credit this aspect of Naples' past for the strength of organized crime here.

Across the street, **Caffè Mexico** (at #86) is an institution known for its espresso, which is served already sweetened—ask for *senza zucchero* if you don't want sugar (pay first, then take receipt to the counter and hand it over). Most Italians agree that Neapolitan coffee is the best anywhere.

• *Walk downhill on...*

Via Toledo: The long, straight street heading downhill from Piazza Dante is Naples' principal shopping drag. It originated as a military road built under Spanish rule (hence the name) in the 16th century. Via Toledo skirted the old town wall to connect the Spanish military headquarters (now the museum where you started this walk) with the Royal Palace (down by the bay, where you're heading). As you stroll, peek into lovely atriums, an ancient urban design feature providing a break from the big street.

After a couple of hundred yards, you'll reach Piazza Sette Settembre. In 1860, from the white marble balcony of the Neo-classical building overlooking the square, the famous revolutionary Giuseppe Garibaldi declared Italy united and Victor Emmanuel II its first king. Only in 1870, a decade later, was the dream of Italian unity fully realized when Rome fell to unification forces.

• *Continue straight on Via Toledo. About three blocks below Piazza Dante and a block past Piazza Sette Settembre, you'll come to Via Maddaloni, which marks the start of the long, straight, narrow street nicknamed...*

Spaccanapoli: Before crossing the street—whose name translates as "split Naples"—look left (toward the train station).
Then look right (to see San Martino hill rising steeply above the center). Since ancient times, this thin street has bisected the city. It changes names several times: Via Maddaloni (as it's called here), Via B. Croce, Via S. Biagio dei Librai, and Via Vicaria Vecchia. We'll return to this intersection later.

• *If you want to abbreviate this walk, turn left here and skip ahead to Part 3. Part 2, described next, is a bit of a detour, and requires backtracking uphill (or a short taxi ride) later. But if you have time, it's worth the effort.*

Part 2: Monumental Naples (Via Toledo, the Spanish Quarter, and Piazza del Plebiscito)

• *We'll detour off of Via Toledo for just a couple of blocks (rejoining it later). At the Spaccanapoli intersection, go right (toward the church facade on the hill, up Via Pasquale Scura). After about 100 yards, you hit a busy intersection. Stop. You're on one of Naples' most colorful open-air market streets...*

Via Pignasecca Market: Snoop around from here if you are so inclined. Then, turn left down Via Pignasecca and stroll this colorful strip. You'll pass meat and fish stalls, produce stands, street-food vendors, and much more. This is a taste of Naples' famous Spanish Quarter, which we'll experience more of later in this walk.

• *Via Pignasecca meets back up with Via Toledo at the square called...*

Piazza Carità: This square, built for an official visit by Hitler to Mussolini in 1938, is full of stern, straight, obedient lines. The big building belonged to an insurance company. (For the best fascist architecture in town, take a slight detour from here: With your back to Via Toledo, leave Piazza Carità downhill on the right-hand corner and walk a block to the Poste e Telegrafi building. There you'll see several government buildings with stirring reliefs singing the praises of lobotomized workers and a totalitarian society.)

In Naples—long a poor and rough city—rather than being heroic, people learn from the cradle the art of survival. The modern memorial statue in the center of the square celebrates Salvo d'Acquisto, a rare hometown hero. In 1943, he was executed after falsely confessing to sabotage...in order to save 22 fellow Italian soldiers from a Nazi revenge massacre.

• *From Piazza Carità, continue south down Via Toledo for a few blocks, looking to your left for more...*

Fascist Architecture (Banks): You can't miss the two big, blocky bank buildings. First comes the chalky-white BNL Bank. A bit farther down, past the Metro, imagine trying to rob the even more imposing Banco di Napoli (Via Toledo 178). Step across the street and check out its architecture: typical fascist arches and reliefs, built to celebrate the bank's 400th anniversary (est. 1539—how old is *your* bank?).

The street here was pedestrianized after the Toledo Metro stop opened in 2012. Now the street is even more popular for strolling, property values have risen, and international brands such as H&M and the Disney Store have moved in.

• *On the next block (at #184) is the...*

Banca Intesa Sanpaolo: This fills an older palace—take a free peek at the opulent atrium. In the entry hall, you can buy a ticket for the **Galleria d'Italia Palazzo Zevallos Stigliano,** a small collection located in the upper two floors. The gallery's only piece worth seeing—on the second floor—is a great late Caravaggio painting. *The Martyrdom of Saint Ursula* shows a terrible scene: His marriage proposal rejected, the king of the Huns shoots an arrow into Ursula's chest. Blood spurts, Ursula is stunned but accepts her destiny sweetly, and Caravaggio himself—far right, his last self-portrait—screams to symbolize the rejection of evil. The rest of the second floor holds opulent chandeliered apartments, a few Neapolitan landscapes, and little else. The first floor has temporary exhibits (€4, Tue-Sun 10:00-18:00, closed Mon; entry includes 40-minute audioguide, a look at old Naples paintings, and a fine WC; Via Toledo 185, tel. 800-454-229, www.palazzozevallos. com).

• *Feeling bold? From here, side-trip uphill a couple of blocks into the...*

Spanish Quarter: This is a classic world of *basso* (low) living. The streets—which were laid out in the 16th century for

the Spanish military barracks outside the city walls—are unbelievably narrow (and cool in summer), and the buildings rise five stories high. In such tight quarters, life—flirting, fighting, playing, and loving—happens in the road. This is *the* cliché of life in Naples, as shown in so many movies.

The Spanish Quarter is Naples at its most characteristic. The shopkeepers are friendly, and the mopeds are bold (watch out). Concerned locals will tug on their lower eyelids, warning you to be wary. Hungry? Pop into a grocery shop and ask the clerk to make you his best prosciutto-and-mozzarella sandwich (the price should be about €4).

• *Return to Via Toledo and work your way down. Near the bottom of the street, on the right, notice the station for the **Centrale funicular.** If you have extra time and enjoy city views, this can take you sweat-free up to the top of San Martino, the hill with a fortress and a monastery/museum looming over town (covered by €1.30 single transit ticket). Across the street is the impressive Galleria Umberto I—but don't go in now, as you'll see it in a minute from the other side.*

For now, just keep heading down the main drag and through the smaller Piazza Trieste e Trento to the immense...

Piazza del Plebiscito: This square celebrates the 1861 vote (*plebiscito,* plebiscite) in which Naples chose to join Italy. Dominating the top of the square is the **Church of San Francesco di Paola,** with its Pantheon-inspired dome and broad, arcing colonnades. If it's open, step inside to ogle the vast interior—a Neoclassical recreation of one of ancient Rome's finest buildings (free, daily 8:30-12:00 & 16:00-19:00).

• *Opposite is the...*

Royal Palace (Palazzo Reale): Having housed Spanish, French, and even Italian royalty, this building displays statues of all those who stayed here. Look for eight kings in the niches, each from a different dynasty (left to right): Norman, German, French, Spanish, Spanish, Spanish, French (Napoleon's brother-in-law), and, finally, Italian—Victor Emmanuel II, King of Savoy. The statues were done at the request of V. E. II's son, so his dad is the most dashing of the group. While you could consider touring the interior, it's relatively unimpressive (described under "Sights in Naples," later).

• *Continue 50 yards past the Royal Palace (toward the trees) to enjoy a...*

Fine Harbor View: While boats busily serve Capri and Sorrento, Mount Vesuvius smolders ominously in the distance. Look back to see the vast "Bourbon red" palace—its color inspired by Pompeii. The hilltop above Piazza del Plebiscito is San Martino, with its Carthusian monastery-turned-museum and Castle of St. Elmo (remember, the Centrale funicular to the top is just across the square and up Via Toledo). This street continues to Naples' romantic harborfront—the fishermen's quarter (Borgo Marinaro)—a fortified island connected to the mainland by a stout causeway, with its fanciful, ancient Castel dell'Ovo (Egg Castle) and trendy harborside restaurants. Farther along the harborfront stretches the Lungomare promenade and Santa Lucia district. (The long harborfront promenade, Via Francesco Caracciolo, is a delightful people-watching scene on balmy nights.)

• *Head back through the piazza and pop into...*

Gran Caffè Gambrinus: This coffee house, facing the piazza, takes you back to the elegance of 1860. It's a classic place to sample a unique Neapolitan treat called *sfogliatella* (crispy scallop shell-shaped pastry filled with sweet ricotta cheese). Or you might prefer the mushroom-shaped, rum-soaked bread-like cakes called *babà*, which come in a huge variety. Stand at the bar *(banco),* pay double to sit *(tavola),* or just wander around as you imagine the café buzzing with the ritzy intellectuals, journalists, and artsy bohemian types who munched on *babà* here during Naples' 19th-century heyday (daily 7:00-24:00, Piazza del Plebiscito 1, tel. 081-417-582).

• *A block away, tucked behind the palace, you can peek inside the Neoclassical...*

Teatro di San Carlo: Built in 1737, 41 years before Milan's La Scala, this is Europe's oldest opera house and Italy's second-most-respected (after La Scala). The theater burned down in 1816, and was rebuilt within the year. Guided 35-minute visits in English basically just show you the fine auditorium with its 184 boxes—each with a big mirror to reflect the candlelight (€6; tours Mon-Sat at 10:30, 11:30, 12:30, 14:30, 15:30, and 16:30; Sun at 10:30, 11:30, and 12:30; tel. 081-797-468, www.teatrosancarlo.it).

Beyond Teatro di San Carlo and the Royal Palace is the huge, harborfront **Castel Nuovo,** which houses government bureaucrats and the **Civic Museum.** It feels like a mostly empty shell, with a couple of dusty halls of Neapolitan art, but the views over the bay from the upper terraces are impressive (€5, Mon-Sat 9:00-19:00, closed Sun, tel. 081-795-7722, www.comune.napoli.it).

Cross the street from Teatro di San Carlo and go through the tall yellow arch into the Victorian iron and glass of the 100-year-old shopping mall, **Galleria Umberto I.** It was built in 1892 to reinvigorate the district after a devastating cholera epidemic occurred here. Gawk up, then walk left to bring you back out on Via Toledo.

• *For Part 3 of this walk, double back up Via Toledo to Piazza Carità, veering right (just above the first big fascist-style building we saw earlier) on Via Morgantini through Piazza Monteoliveto. Cross the busy street, then angle up Calata Trinità Maggiore to the fancy column at the top of the hill. (To avoid the backtracking and uphill walk, catch a €10 taxi to the Church of Gesù Nuovo—JAY-zoo noo-OH-voh.)*

Part 3: Spaccanapoli Back to the Station

You're back at the straight-as-a-Greek-arrow Spaccanapoli, formerly the main thoroughfare of the Greek city of Neapolis.

• *Stop at...*

Piazza Gesù Nuovo: This square is marked by a towering 18th-century Baroque monument to the Counter-Reformation. Although the Jesuit order was powerful in Naples because of its Spanish heritage, locals never attacked Protestants here with the full fury of the Spanish Inquisition.

If you'd like, you can visit two bulky old churches, starting with the dark, fortress-like, 17th-century **Church of Gesù Nuovo,** followed by the simpler **Church of Santa Chiara** (in the courtyard across the street). Both are described in more detail later, under "Sights in Naples."

• *After touring the churches, continue along the main drag. Since this is a university district, you'll see lots of students and bookstores. This neighborhood is also famously superstitious. Look for incense-burning women with carts full of good-luck charms for sale.*

Farther down Spaccanapoli—passing Palazzo Venezia, the embassy of Venice to Naples when both were independent powers—you'll see the next square...

Piazza San Domenico Maggiore: This square is marked by an ornate 17th-century monument built to thank God for ending the plague. From this square, detour left along the right side of the castle-like church, then follow yellow signs, taking the first right and walking one block to the remarkable **Cappella Sansevero.** This Baroque chapel is well worth visiting (described later, under "Sights in Naples").

• *After touring the chapel, return to Via B. Croce (a.k.a. Spaccanapoli), turn left, and continue your cultural scavenger hunt. At the intersection of Via Nilo, find the...*

Statue of the Nile (on the left): A reminder of the multi-ethnic make-up of Greek Neapolis, this statue is in what was the Egyptian quarter. Locals like to call this statue *The Body of Naples*, with the overflowing cornucopia symbolizing the abundance of their fine city. (I once asked a Neapolitan man to describe the local women, who are famous for their beauty, in one word. He replied simply, "Abundant.") This intersection is considered the center of old Naples.

• *Directly opposite the statue, between the two doors of Bar Nilo, is the...*

"Chapel of Maradona": The small "chapel" on the wall is dedicated to Diego Maradona, a soccer star who played for Naples in the 1980s. Locals consider soccer almost a religion, and this guy was practically a deity. You can even see a "hair of Diego" and a teardrop from the city when he went to another team for more money. Unfortunately, his reputation has since been sullied by problems he's had with organized crime, drugs, and police. Perhaps inspired by Maradona's example, the coffee bar has posted a quadrilingual sign (though, strangely, not in English) threatening that those who take a picture without buying a cup of coffee may find their camera damaged...*Capisce?* (Note that this "chapel" is removable—if it's raining or they're just feeling grumpy, it may be gone.)

• *As you continue, you'll begin to see shops selling...*

Presepi (Nativity Scenes): Just as many Americans keep an eye out year-round for Christmas-tree ornaments, Italians regularly add pieces to the family *presepe*, the centerpiece of their holiday decorations. Stop after a few blocks at the tiny square, where Via San Gregorio Armeno leads left into a colorful district with the highest concentration of shops selling fantastic *presepi* and their tiny components, including figurines caricaturing local politicians and celebrities. Also in this neighborhood is the underground Napoli Sotteranea archaeological site (described later, under "Sights in Naples").

• *Back on Spaccanapoli, as Via B. Croce becomes Via S. Biagio dei Librai, notice the...*

Gold and Silver Shops: Some say stolen jewelry ends up here, is melted down immediately, and gets resold in some other form as soon as it cools. At #95, find the Compro Oro ("I Buy Gold") shop. This is one of many pawn shops that have appeared recently, in concert with Italy's economic tough times. At #81, the Ospedale delle Bambole (Doll Hospital) heals dolls that have been loved to pieces, and also sells restored classics.

• *Cross busy Via Duomo. If you have time and aren't already churched out, consider detouring five minutes north (left) up Via Duomo to visit*

Naples' **Duomo;** *just around the corner is the* **Pio Monte della Miseri-cordia Church,** *with a fine Caravaggio painting (both described later, under "Sights in Naples"). Afterwards, continue straight along Via Vicaria Vecchia. As you stroll, ponder Naples' vibrant...*

Street Life, Past and Present: Here along Via Vicaria Vecchia, the street and side-street scenes intensify. The area is said to be a center of the Camorra (organized crime), but as a tourist, you won't notice. Paint a picture with these thoughts: Naples has the most intact street plan of any ancient Greek or Roman city. Imagine this city during those times (and retain these images as you visit Pompeii), with streetside shop fronts that close up after dark, and private homes on upper floors. What you see today is just one more page in a 2,000-year-old story of a city: all kinds of meetings, beatings, and cheatings; kisses, near misses, and little-boy pisses.

You name it, it occurs right on the streets today, as it has since ancient times. People ooze from crusty corners. Black-and-

white death announcements add to the clutter on the walls. Widows sell cigarettes from buckets. For a peek behind the scenes in the shade of wet laundry, venture down a few side streets. Buy two carrots as a gift for the woman on the fifth floor, if she'll lower her bucket to pick them up. The neighborhood action seems best at about 18:00.

A few blocks on, at the tiny fenced-in triangle of greenery, hang out for a few minutes to just observe the crazy motorbike action and teen scene.

• *From here, veer right onto Via Forcella (which leads to the busy boulevard that takes you to Centrale Station). A block down, a tiny, fenced-in traffic island protects a chunk of the ancient Greek wall of Neapolis. Turn right here on Via Pietro Colletta, walk 40 yards, and step into the North Pole, at the...*

Polo Nord Gelateria: The oldest *gelateria* in Naples has had four generations of family working here since 1931. Before you order, sample a few flavors, including their *bacio* or "kiss" flavor (chocolate and hazelnut)—all are made fresh daily. Low-sugar and soy ice cream are also available (Via Pietro Colletta 41). Via Pietro Colletta leads past two of Napoli's most competitive **pizzerias** (see "Eating in Naples," later) to Corso Umberto I.

• *Turn left on the grand boulevard-like Corso Umberto I. From here to Centrale Station, it's at least a 10-minute walk (if you're tired, hop on a bus; they all go to the station). To finish the walk, continue on Corso Umberto I—past a gauntlet of purse/CD/sunglasses salesmen and shady characters hawking stolen mobile phones—to the vast, ugly Piazza Garibaldi. On the far side is the station. You made it.*

Sights in Naples

Churches on or near Spaccanapoli

These churches are linked—in this order—on Part 3 of my self-guided walk, earlier.

▲Church of Gesù Nuovo

This church's unique pyramid-grill facade survives from a fortified 15th-century noble palace. Step inside for a brilliant Neapolitan Baroque interior. The second chapel on the right features a much-adored **statue of St. Giuseppe Moscati** (1880-1927), a Christian doctor famous for helping the poor. In 1987, Moscati became the first modern doctor to be canonized. Sit and watch a steady stream of Neapolitans taking turns to kiss and touch the altar, then hold the good doctor's highly polished hand.

Continue on to the third chapel and enter the **Sale Moscati.** Look high on the walls of this long room to see hundreds of "Ex Votos"—tiny red-and-silver plaques of thanksgiving for prayers answered with the help of St. Moscati (each has a symbol of the ailment cured). Naples' practice of using Ex Votos, while incorporated into its Catholic rituals, goes back to its pagan Greek roots. Rooms from Moscati's nearby apartment are on display, and a glass case shows possessions and photos of the great doctor. As you leave the Sale Moscati, notice the big bomb casing that hangs in the left corner. It fell through the church's dome in 1943, but caused almost no damage...yet another miracle.

Cost and Hours: Free, daily 7:00-13:00 & 16:00-19:30, Piazza del Gesù Nuovo, www.gesunuovo.it.

Church of Santa Chiara

Dating from the 14th century, this church is from a period of French royal rule under the Angevin dynasty. Consider the stark contrast between this church (Gothic) and the Gesù Nuovo (Baroque), across the street. Inside, notice the huge inlaid-marble Angevin coat of arms on the floor. The faded Trinity on the back wall (on the right as you face the door), shows a dove representing the Holy Spirit between the heads of God the Father and Christ (c. 1414). This is an example of the fine frescoes that once covered the walls. Most were stuccoed over during Baroque times or destroyed in 1943 by Allied bombs. The altar is adorned with four finely carved Gothic tombs of Angevin kings. A chapel stacked with Bourbon royalty is just to the right.

Cost and Hours: Free, daily 7:00-13:00 & 16:30-20:00, Piazza del Gesù Nuovo. Its tranquil cloistered courtyard, around back, is not worth its €6 entry fee.

▲▲Cappella Sansevero

This small chapel is a Baroque explosion mourning the body of Christ, who lies on a soft pillow under an incredibly realistic veil. It's also the personal chapel of Raimondo de Sangro, an eccentric Freemason, containing his tomb and the tombs of his family. Like other 18th-century Enlightenment figures, Raimondo was a wealthy man of letters, scientist and inventor, and patron of the arts—and he was also a grand master of the Freemasons of the Kingdom of Naples. His chapel—filled with Freemason symbolism—is a complex ensemble, with statues representing virtues such as self-control, religious zeal, and the Freemason philosophy of freedom through enlightenment. Though it's a pricey private enterprise, the chapel is worth a visit.

Cost and Hours: €7, buy tickets at office at the corner, Mon and Wed-Sat 10:00-18:00, Sun 10:00-13:30, closed Tue, last entry 20 minutes before closing, no photos, Via de Sanctis 19, tel. 081-551-8470, www.museosansevero.it. Good English explanations are posted throughout; when you buy your ticket, pick up the free floor plan, which identifies each of the statues lining the nave.

Visiting the Chapel: Study the incredible *Veiled Christ* in the center. Carved out of marble, it's like no other statue I've seen (by Giuseppe "Howdeedoodat" Sammartino, 1753). The Christian message (Jesus died for our salvation) is accompanied by a Freemason message (the veil represents how the body and ego are obstacles to real spiritual freedom). As you walk from Christ's feet to his head, notice how the expression on Jesus' face goes from suffering to peace.

Raimondo's mom and dad are buried on either side of the **main altar.** To the right of the altar, marking his father's tomb, a statue representing *Despair* or *Disillusion* struggles with a marble rope net (carved out of a single piece of stone), symbolic of a troubled mind. The flames on the head of the winged boy represent human intellect—more Freemason symbolism, showing how knowledge frees the human mind. To the left of the main altar is a statue of *Modesty,* marking the tomb of Raimondo's mother (who died after his birth, and was only 20). The veiled woman fingers a broken tablet, symbolizing an interrupted life.

Raimondo de Sangro himself lies buried in a side altar (on the right). Among his inventions was the deep-green pigment used on the ceiling fresco. The inlaid M. C. Escher-esque maze on the floor around de Sangro's tomb is another Freemason reminder of how the quest for knowledge gets you out of the maze of life. This tilework once covered the floor of the entire chapel.

Your Sansevero finale is downstairs: two mysterious...**skeletons.** Perhaps another of the mad inventor's fancies: Inject a corpse with a fluid to fossilize the veins so that they'll survive the body's decomposition. While that's the legend, recent investigations have shown that the veins were artificial, and the models were created to illustrate how the circulatory system works.

▲Duomo

Naples' historic cathedral, built by imported French Anjou kings in the 14th century, boasts a breathtaking Neo-Gothic facade. Step into the vast interior to see the mix of styles along the side chapels—from pointy Gothic arches to rounded Renaissance ones to gilded Baroque decor.

Cost and Hours: Free, daily 8:30-13:30 & 14:30-20:00, Via Duomo.

Visiting the Church: Explore the two largest side-chapels—each practically a church in its own right. On the left, the Chapel of St. Restituta stands on the site of the original, early-Christian church that predated the cathedral (at the far end, you can pay €1.50 to see its sixth-century baptismal font under mosaics, and go downstairs to see its even earlier foundations; chapel open Mon-Sat 8:30-12:30 & 16:30-18:30, Sun 8:30-13:00). On the right is the Chapel of San Gennaro—dedicated to the beloved patron saint of Naples—decorated with silver busts of centuries of bishops, and seven paintings done on bronze.

Back out in the main nave, the altar at the front is ringed by carved wooden seats, filled three times a year by clergy to witness the Miracle of the Blood. Thousands of Neapolitans cram into this church for a peek at two tiny vials with the dried blood of St. Gennaro. As the clergy roots—or even jeers—for the miracle to occur, the blood temporarily liquefies. Neapolitans take this ritual with deadly seriousness, and believe that if the blood remains solid, it's terrible luck for the city. Sure enough, on the rare occasion that the miracle fails, locals can point to a terrible event soon after—such as an earthquake or an eruption of Mount Vesuvius.

The stairs beneath the altar take you to a crypt with the relics of St. Gennaro and (across the room) a statue of the bishop who rescued the relics from a rival town and returned them to Naples.

Pio Monte della Misericordia

Art lovers come to this small church (near the Duomo, and run by a charitable foundation) to appreciate one of the best works by Caravaggio, *The Seven Works of Mercy,* which hangs over the main altar. In one crowded canvas, the great early-Baroque artist illustrates seven virtues: burying the dead (the man carrying a corpse by the ankles), visiting the imprisoned, feeding the hungry (Pero breastfeeding her starving father—a scene from a famous Roman story), sheltering the homeless (a pilgrim on the Camino de Santiago, with his floppy hat, negotiates with an innkeeper), caring for the sick, clothing the naked (St. Martin offers part of his cloak to the injured man in the foreground), and giving drink to the thirsty

(Samson chugs from a jawbone in the background)—all of them set in a dark Neapolitan alley and watched over by Mary, Jesus, and a pair of angels. Caravaggio painted this work in Naples in 1607, while in exile from Rome, where he had been sentenced to death for killing a man in a duel. Your ticket also lets you in to the foundation's pleasant upper-floor museum, with some minor Neapolitan paintings.

Cost and Hours: €6, includes audioguide, Thu-Tue 9:00-14:30, closed Wed, Via dei Tribunali 253, tel. 081-446-944, www.piomontedellamisericordia.it.

In the City Center
Royal Palace (Palazzo Reale)
Facing Piazza del Plebiscito, this huge, lavish palace welcomes the public. The palace's grand Neoclassical staircase leads up to a floor with 30 plush rooms. You'll follow a one-way route (with some English descriptions) featuring the palace theater, paintings by "the Caravaggio Imitators," Neapolitan tapestries, fine inlaid-stone tabletops, chandeliers, gilded woodwork, and more. The rooms do feel quite grand, but they lack the personality and sense of importance of Europe's better palaces. Don't miss the huge, tapestry-laden Hercules Hall. On the way out, stop into the chapel, with a fantastic nativity scene—a commotion of 18th-century ceramic figurines.

Cost and Hours: €4, includes painfully dry audioguide, Thu-Tue 9:00-20:00, closed Wed, last entry one hour before closing, tel. 848-800-288.

▲Napoli Sotterranea
This archaeological site, a manmade underground maze of passage-ways and ruins from Greek and Roman times, can only be toured with a guide. You'll descend 121 steps under the modern city to explore two different underground areas. One is the old Greek tuff quarry used to build the city of Neapolis, which was later converted into an immense cistern by the Romans. The other is an excavated portion of the Greco-Roman theater that once seated 6,000 people. It's clear that this space has been encroached upon by modern development—some current residents' windows literally look down into the theater ruins. The tour involves a lot of stairs, as well as a long, narrow 20-inch-wide walkway—lit only by candlelight—that uses an ancient water channel (a heavyset person could not comfortably fit through this, and claustrophobes will be miserable). Although there's not much to actually see, the experience is fascinating and includes a little history from World War II—when the quarry/cistern was turned into a shelter to protect locals from American bombs.

Cost and Hours: €9.30; includes 1.5-hour tour. Visits in

English are offered daily at 10:00, 12:00, 14:00, 16:00, and 18:00. Bring a light sweater. Tel. 081-296-944, www.napolisotterranea. org.

Getting There: The site is at Piazza San Gaetano 68, along Via dei Tribunali. It's a 10-minute walk from the Archaeological Museum, and just a couple of blocks uphill from Spaccanapoli's statue of the Nile. The entrance is immediately to the left of the Church of San Paolo Maggiore (look for the *Sotterranea* signs).

Porta Nolana Open-Air Fish Market

Naples' fish market squirts and stinks as it has for centuries under the Porta Nolana (gate in the city wall), immediately in front of the

Napoli Porta Nolana Circumvesuviana station and four long blocks from Centrale Station. Of the town's many boisterous outdoor markets, this will net you the most photos and memories. From Piazza Nolana, wander under the medieval gate and take your first left down Vico Sopramuro, enjoying this wild and entirely edible cultural scavenger hunt (Tue-Sun 8:00-14:00, closed Mon).

Two other markets with more clothing and fewer fish are at Piazza Capuana (several blocks northwest of Centrale Station and tumbling down Via Sant'Antonio Abate, Mon-Sat 8:00-18:00, Sun 9:00-13:00) and a similar cobbled shopping zone along Via Pignasecca (just off Via Toledo, west of Piazza Carità).

Lungomare *Passeggiata*

Each evening, relaxed and romantic Neapolitans in the mood for a scenic harborside stroll do their *vasche* (laps) along the inviting Lungomare promenade. To join in this elegant people-watching scene (best after 19:00), stroll about 15 minutes from Piazza del Plebiscito along Via Nazario Sauro.

Detour out along the fortified causeway to poke around Borgo Marinaro ("fishermen's quarter"), with its striking Castel dell'Ovo and a trendy restaurant scene (see "Eating in Naples," later), where you can dine amidst yachts with a view of Vesuvius. This is known as the Santa Lucia district because this is where the song "Santa Lucia" was first performed. (The song is probably so famous in America because immigrants from Naples sang it to remember the old country.) Beyond that stretches the Lungomare, along Via Francesco Caracciolo. Taxi home or retrace your steps back to the old center.

On San Martino

The ultimate view overlooking Naples, its bay, and the volcano is from the hill called San Martino, just above (and west of) the city center. Up top you'll find a mighty fortress (which charges for entry but offers the best views from its ramparts) and the adjacent monastery-turned-museum. While neither of these sights is exciting in its own right, the views are. And the surrounding neighborhood (especially Piazza Fuga) has a classy "uptown" vibe compared to the gritty city-center streets below. Cheapskates can enjoy the views for free from the benches on the square in front of the monastery.

Getting There: From Via Toledo, the Spanish Quarter gradually climbs up San Martino's lower slopes, before steep paths take you up the rest of the way. But the easiest way to ascend San Martino is by funicular. Three different funicular lines lead from lower Naples to the hilltop: the Centrale line from near the bottom of Via Toledo, the Montesanto line from the Metro stop of the same name (near the top end of Via Toledo), and the Chiaia line from farther out, near Piazza Amadeo (all three are covered by any regular local transit ticket). Ride any of these three up to the end of the line. All three lines converge within a few blocks at the top of the hill—Centrale and Chiaia wind up at opposite ends of the charming Piazza Fuga, while Montesanto terminates a bit closer to the fortress and museum. Leaving any of the funiculars, head uphill, carefully tracking signs for *Castel S. Elmo* and *Museo di San Martino* (strategically placed escalators make the climb easier). You'll reach the castle first, and then the monastery/museum (both about 10 minutes' walk from Piazza Fuga).

Castel Sant'Elmo

While it's little more than an empty husk with a decent modern art museum, this 16th-century, Spanish-built, star-shaped fortress boasts commanding views over the city and the entire Bay of Naples. Buy your ticket at the booth, then ride the elevator up to the upper courtyard and climb up to the ramparts for a slow circle to enjoy the 360-degree views. In the middle of the yard is the likeable little Museo del Novecento, a gallery of works by 20th-century Neapolitan artists (last entry at 18:00, covered by same ticket); the castle also hosts temporary exhibits.

Cost and Hours: €5, open Wed-Mon 8:30-19:30, closed Tue, last entry one hour before closing, hours can be unreliable, Via Tito Angelini 22, tel. 081-229-4401.

▲San Martino Carthusian Monastery and Museum (Certosa e Museo di San Martino)

The monastery, founded in 1325 and dissolved in the early 1800s, is now a sprawling museum with several parts. The square out front has city views nearly as good as the ones you'll pay to see from inside, and a few cafés angling for your business.

NAPLES

Cost and Hours: €6, audioguide-€5, Thu-Tue 8:30-19:30, closed Wed, last entry one hour before closing, Largo San Martino 8, tel. 081-229-4502, http://museosanmartino.campaniabeniculturali.it.

Visiting the Monastery and Museum: If you want to tour the place, buy your ticket and head into the complex (which has some English information). Step into the church, a Baroque explosion with beautifully decorated chapels. Around the humble cloister are a variety of museum exhibits. The Naval Museum has nautical paintings, model boats, and giant ceremonial gondolas. In an adjacent hall is an excellent collection of *presepi* (nativity scenes), both life-size and miniature, including a spectacular one by Michele Cucinello—the best I've seen in this *presepi*-crazy city. Beyond that is the larger garden cloister, ringed with a painting gallery (with lots of antique maps and artifacts of old Naples), and an entrance to a pretty view terrace.

On Capodimonte

Another hilltop, about a mile due north from the Archaeological Museum, is home to Naples' top art museum—the **Museo di Capodimonte.** Its three floors of art include works by Raphael, Titian, Caravaggio, and Bellini. While most visitors to Naples prefer to focus on the city's uniquely vibrant street life, characteristic churches, and remarkable ancient artifacts—and there are far better art museums elsewhere in Italy—art lovers with some time to spare may find a visit to Capodimonte worth the trip. While bus #C63 does run to Capodimonte from Piazza Dante and the Archaeological Museum, it's easier to take a taxi (about €8-10 from downtown).

Cost and Hours: €7.50, Thu-Tue 8:30-19:30, closed Wed, last entry one hour before closing, Via Miano 2, tel. 081-749-9111.

Sleeping in Naples

As an alternative to intense Naples, most travelers prefer to sleep in mellow Sorrento, just over an hour away. But, if needed, here are a few good options. The prices listed are typical for high season (spring and late fall). In this business-oriented (rather than tourist-oriented) city, prices are particularly soft during the slow summer months (July-Sept).

Near Via Toledo and Spaccanapoli

$$$ Decumani Hotel de Charme is a classy oasis tucked away on a residential lane in the very heart of the city, just off Spaccanapoli. While the neighborhood is Naples-dingy, the 22 rooms—filling an elegant 18th-century palace with a gorgeous breakfast room—

Sleep Code

(€1 = about $1.30, country code: 39)

S = Single, **D** = Double/Twin, **T** = Triple, **Q** = Quad, **b** = bathroom, **s** = shower only. Unless otherwise noted, credit cards are accepted, English is spoken, and breakfast is included. Many cities in Italy levy a hotel tax of about €2 per person, per night, which must be paid in cash (not included in the rates I've quoted).

To help you sort easily through these listings, I've divided the accommodations into three categories based on the price for a standard double room with bath:

$$$ Higher Priced—Most rooms €130 or more.

$$ Moderately Priced—Most rooms between €90-130.

$ Lower Priced—Most rooms €90 or less.

Prices can change without notice; verify the hotel's current rates online or by email.

are an inviting retreat (standard Db-€134, bigger deluxe Db-€15 more, rates soft—check website for deals, air-con, elevator, free Wi-Fi, Via San Giovanni Maggiore Pignatelli 15—this lane is one street towards the station from Via Santa Chiara, second floor, tel. 081-551-8188, www.decumani.com, info@decumani.com).

$$$ Hotel Piazza Bellini is a newish hotel with 48 stripped-down-minimalist but comfy rooms surrounding a quiet courtyard. Two blocks below the Archaeological Museum and just off the lively Piazza Bellini, it offers modern sanity in the city center (generally Sb-€120, Db-€170, less if slow, bi-level "superior" Db-€20 more, extra bed-€20, air-con, elevator, free Internet access and Wi-Fi, Via Santa Maria di Constantinopoli 101, close to Metro: Dante, tel. 081-451-732, www.hotelpiazzabellini.com, info@hotelpiazzabellini.com).

$$ Chiaja Hotel de Charme, with the same owner as the Decumani (listed earlier), rents 33 less expensive rooms on the upscale Via Chiaia pedestrian shopping drag near Piazza del Plebiscito (smaller standard Db with interior view-€119, bigger Db with view of pedestrian street-€139, air-con, elevator, free Wi-Fi, Via Chiaia 216, first floor, tel. 081-415-555, www.hotelchiaia.it, info@hotelchiaia.it, Pietro Fusella).

$$ Art Resort Galleria Umberto has 15 rooms in two different buildings inside the Umberto I shopping gallery at the bottom of Via Toledo, just off Piazza del Plebiscito. This genteel-feeling place gilds the lily, with an aristocratic setting and decor but older bathrooms. Consider paying €20 extra for a room overlooking the gallery (cheapest non-view Db-€109-120, elevator, air-con, free Wi-Fi, Galleria Umberto 83, fourth floor—ask at booth for coin to operate elevator if needed, tel. 081-497-6224, www.artresortgalleriaumberto.it, info@artresortgalleriaumberto.it).

$$ Hotel Il Convento, with 14 small but comfortable rooms with balconies, is a good choice for those who want to sleep in the gnarly, tight tangle of lanes called the Spanish Quarter—quintessential Naples. While the neighborhood can feel off-putting after dark, it's not especially unsafe. You're only a couple of short blocks off the main Via Toledo drag, and heavy-duty windows help block out some—but not all—of the scooter noise and church bells. A rare haven in this characteristic corner of town, it's in all the guidebooks (Sb-€80, Db-€120, Tb-€130, Qb-€160, €10-20 less if you prepay, elevator, air-con, free Wi-Fi, Via Speranzella 137A, tel. 081-403-977, www.hotelilconvento.com, info@hotelilconvento.com).

Near the Train Station

Although rates here are cheaper and it's very handy to the station, this area is relatively inconvenient for sightseeing and dining, less characteristic than the areas described earlier, and can feel unnerving—especially after dark.

$ Grand Hotel Europa, a gem on a seedy street right next to the station, has 89 decent rooms whimsically decorated with not-quite-right reproductions of famous paintings (Sb-€65, Db-€85, Tb-€109, book direct and ask for 15 percent Rick Steves discount off these prices or check website for special deals, air-con, elevator, free guest computer, free Wi-Fi near reception, restaurant, Corso Meridionale 14, tel. 081-267-511, www.grandhoteleuropa.com, info@grandhoteleuropa.com, well-run by Claudio). To find the hotel, exit the station on the north side, past track 5. You'll turn left and a right around a green *Polfer* sign, then exit through a gate. The hotel is across the street and a few doors down to the right.

$ Hotel Suite Esedra, with 17 small but tasteful rooms, is an affordable four-star charmer on a tiny square off busy Corso Umberto I, located just outside of the station-neighborhood sleaze (Sb-€60, Db-€80, these prices if you book direct and mention this book, air-con, elevator, free Wi-Fi, 10-minute walk from the station at Via Arnaldo Cantani 12—across the Corso from the Church of Santa Maria Egiziaca, tel. 081-287-451, www.hotelsuiteesedranapoli.it, info@hotelsuiteesedranapoli.it, Alessandro).

$ Hotel Potenza offers a rare bit of security and peace right on Piazza Garibaldi, 100 yards in front of the station. Its 26 pleasant rooms have good windows that help block out the bustle (Sb-€50, Db-€70, Tb-€75, Qb-€92, air-con, no elevator, free Wi-Fi, 100

NAPLES

Naples Hotels & Restaurants Key

❶ Decumani Hotel de Charme
❷ Hotel Piazza Bellini &
   La Stanza del Gusto
❸ Chiaja Hotel de Charme
❹ Art Resort Galleria Umberto
❺ Hotel Il Convento
❻ Hotel Suite Esedra
❼ Antica Pizzeria da Michele &
   Pizzeria Trianon
❽ Gino Sorbillo Pizzeria
❾ Pizzeria di Matteo

❿ Pizzeria I Decumani &
   Trattoria Campagnola
⓫ Ecomesarà
⓬ Osteria il Garum
⓭ Valù
⓮ To Trattoria da Nennella
⓯ Caffetteria Angela
⓰ Salumeria Pasquale Carrino
⓱ Polo Nord Gelateria
⓲ Supermarket
⓳ Laundry

yards in front of the station at Piazza Garibaldi 120, tel. 081-286-330, www.hotelpotenza.com, info@hotelpotenza.com, Valenzano family).

In Chiaia, Farther Out

$$ Pinto-Storey Hotel seems a world away from the bustle of the city center. With 16 straightforward rooms in a relatively upscale neighborhood (three Metro stops from the train station), the hotel has an old-time charm (Sb-€78, Db-€98, Tb-€139, these prices if you book direct and mention this book, air-con-€8, elevator, expensive Wi-Fi, across the square from Metro line 2's Amedeo stop at Via Martucci 72, tel. 081-681-260, www.pintostorey.it, info@pintostorey.it).

Eating in Naples

Cheap and Famous Pizza

Naples is the birthplace of pizza. Its pizzerias bake just the right combination of fresh dough, mozzarella, and tomatoes in traditional wood-burning ovens. You can head for the famous, venerable places (I've listed five below), but these can have a long line stretching out the door, and a half-hour wait for a table. If you want to skip the hassle, just ask your hotel for directions to the neighborhood pizzeria. An average one-person pie costs €4-6; most places offer both take-out and eat-in.

Near the Station

These two pizzerias—the most famous—are both a few long blocks from the train station, and at the end of my "Slice of Neapolitan Life" self-guided walk.

Antica Pizzeria da Michele is for pizza purists. Filled with locals (and tourists), it serves just two varieties: *margherita* (tomato sauce and mozzarella) and *marinara* (tomato sauce, oregano, and garlic, no cheese). Come early to sit and watch the pizza artists in action. A pizza with beer costs €6-7. As this place is often jammed with a long line, arrive early or late to get a seat. If there's a mob, head inside to get a number. If it's just too crowded to wait, the less-exceptional Pizzeria Trianon (described next) generally has room (Mon-Sat 10:30-24:00, closed Sun; look for the vertical red *Antica Pizzeria* sign at the intersection of Via Pietro Colletta and Via Cesare Sersale at #1; tel. 081-553-9204).

Pizzeria Trianon, across the street and left a few doors, has been da Michele's archrival since 1923. It offers more choices, slightly higher prices (€5-7), air-conditioning, and a cozier atmosphere. For less chaos, head upstairs. While waiting for your meal, you can survey the transformation of a humble wad of dough into a smoldering bubbly feast in their entryway pizza kitchen (daily 11:00-15:30 & 19:00-23:00, Via Pietro Colletta 42, tel. 081-553-9426, Giuseppe).

On Via dei Tribunali

This street, which runs a couple of blocks north of Spaccanapoli, is home to several pizzerias that are more convenient to sightseeing. Three in particular are on all the "best pizza in Naples" lists...as you'll learn the hard way if you show up at peak mealtimes, when huge mobs crowd outside the front door waiting for a table. **Gino Sorbillo** is a local favorite (closed Sun, Via dei Tribunali 32—don't confuse this with his relatives' similarly named places on the same street, tel. 081-446-643). At **Pizzeria di Matteo,** people waiting out front snack on €0.50 croquettes *(crocché),* sold at the little window (closed Sun, Via dei Tribunali 94, tel. 081-455-262). **Pizzeria I Decumani** has a bit nicer seating and is open seven days a week (facing Piazza San Gaetano at Via dei Tribunali 58, tel. 081-557-1309).

Restaurants

If you want a full meal rather than a pizza, consider these options, which I've organized by neighborhood.

Near Spaccanapoli and Via Toledo

Ecomesarà serves up Neapolitan and *meridionale* (southern Italian) dishes in a modern setting just below the Santa Chiara cloister, a long block south of Spaccanapoli. The atmosphere is mellow, modern, and international. Cristiano and his staff are happy to explain the menu, which refreshingly dispenses with the traditional Italian *primi/secondi* distinction. Cristiano—who abides by the Slow Food ethic—explains that separate *contorni* (vegetable sides) aren't necessary because *all* of their dishes have vegetables (€9-16 main courses, Tue-Sun 13:00-15:00 & 19:30-23:00, closed Mon, Via Santa Chiara 49, tel. 081-1925-9353).

Trattoria Campagnola is a classic family place with a daily home-cooking-style chalkboard menu on the back wall, mama busy cooking in the back, and wine on tap. Here you can venture away from pastas, be experimental with a series of local dishes, and not go wrong (€7 main courses, Wed-Mon 12:00-16:00 & 19:00-23:00, closed Tue, between the famous pizzerias at Via Tribunali 47, tel. 081-459-034 but no reservations).

Osteria il Garum is great if you'd like to eat on a classic Neapolitan square. It's named for the ancient fish sauce that was widely used in Roman cooking. These days, mild-mannered Luigi and his staff inject their pricey local cuisine with centuries of tradition, served in a cozy split-level cellar or outside on a covered terrace facing a neighborhood church. It's just between Via Toledo and Spaccanapoli, a short walk from the Church of Gesù Nuovo (€9-13 pastas, €14-17 *secondi,* daily 12:00-15:30 & 19:00-23:30, Piazza Monteoliveto 2A, tel. 081-542-3228).

Valù, with a modern red-and-black color scheme and a wine-bar vibe, sits sane and romantic in the colorful and rowdy Spanish Quarter just a block off Via Toledo. This *risotteria* specializes in risotto (which is not a local dish), serving 20 different variations. Choose between the interior or a few outdoor tables along a tight alley (€10-12 risottos, €8-16 meat dishes, Mon-Sat 12:30-15:00 & 19:00-24:00, closed Sun, Vico Lungo del Gelso 80, up alley directly opposite Banco di Napoli entrance, tel. 081-038-1139).

Trattoria da Nennella is fun-loving chaos, with red-shirted waiters barking orders, a small festival anytime someone puts a tip in the bucket, and the fruit course served in plastic bidets. There's one price—€12 per person—and you choose three courses plus a fruit. House wine is served in tiny plastic cups, the crowd is ready for fun, and the food's good. It's buried in the Spanish Quarter. You can sit indoors, or on a cobbled terrace under a trellis (closed Sun, leave Via Toledo a block down from the BNL bank and walk up Vico Teatro Nuovo three blocks to the corner of Vico Lungo Teatro Nuovo, Vico Lungo Teatro Nuovo 103, tel. 081-414-338 but no reservations).

Near the Archaeological Museum

La Stanza del Gusto, two blocks downhill from the museum, tackles food creatively and injects crusty Naples with a little modern color and irreverence. The downstairs is casual, trendy, and playful, while the upstairs is more refined yet still polka-dotted (€5-8 *panini,* €10-15 *secondi;* fixed-price meals: €35 five-course vegetarian, €65 seven-course meat; Tue-Sat 12:00-15:30 & 19:30-23:30, closed Sun-Mon, Via Santa Maria di Constantinopoli 100, tel. 081-401-578).

Caffetteria Angela is a fun little eating complex: coffee bar;

Getting Around the Region

To connect Naples, Sorrento, and the Amalfi Coast, you can travel on land by train, bus, and taxi. Whenever possible, consider taking a boat—it's faster, cooler, and more scenic, and you can take coastline photos that you can't get from land. For specifics, check the "Connections" sections of the Naples, Sorrento, and Amalfi Coast chapters. Confirm times and prices locally.

By Circumvesuviana Train: This useful commuter train—popular with locals, tourists, and pickpockets—links Naples, Herculaneum, Pompeii, and Sorrento. At Naples' Centrale Station, follow *Circumvesuviana* signs downstairs and down the corridor to the Circumvesuviana ticket windows and turnstiles. When you buy your ticket, ask which track your train will depart from ("*Quale binario*?"; KWAH-lay bee-NAH-ree-oh). Insert your ticket at the turnstiles and find your platform (down another level).

Circumvesuviana tickets are covered by the Campania ArteCard (see page 6), but not railpasses. All-day Circumvesuviana tickets are available, but—unless you're making several stops on a long round-trip—aren't worth considering, except on weekends, when they're nearly half-price (€12 Mon-Fri, €6.50 "weekend pass" available Sat-Sun). For schedules, see www.vesuviana.it.

If you're heading to **Pompeii** or **Herculaneum,** take any Circumvesuviana train marked *Sorrento*—they all stop at both places. Sorrento-bound trains depart twice hourly, and take about 20 minutes to reach Ercolano Scavi (for the Herculaneum ruins, €2.20 one-way), 40 minutes to reach Pompei Scavi-Villa Misteri (for the Pompeii ruins, €2.90 one-way), and 70 minutes to reach **Sorrento**, the end of the line (€4.20 one-way). Express trains to Sorrento marked *DD* (6/day) reach Sorrento 15 minutes sooner (and also stop at Herculaneum and Pompeii).

As you board, double-check with a local that the train goes to Sorrento, as the Circumvesuviana has several lines that branch out to other destinations. When returning to Naples on the Circumvesuviana, remember that the name of the Circumvesuviana stop at Centrale Station is "Garibaldi." Back in Naples, you can use your Circumvesuviana ticket to cover all public transit within three hours of validation (no need to validate again).

Be on guard: Many readers report being ripped off on the Circumvesuviana (see "Theft Alert," page 8).

If you're **coming from Rome,** note that a different (non-Circumvesuviana) train—run by the national rail company—goes from Rome to Naples, then continues to the ugly modern city of Pompei. But there is almost no reason to go to Pompei city, where you'll face a long walk to the actual site. It's better to simply get off at Naples' Centrale Station and transfer to the Circumvesuviana (described above). The Pompei city train station is useful only if you need to travel directly between the ruins and Salerno (roughly hourly, 20 minutes) or Paestum (4 trains/day, 1 hour).

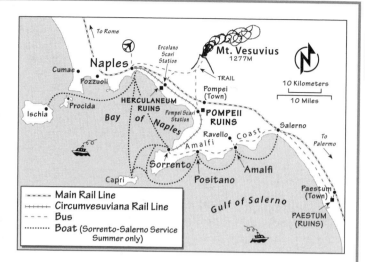

By Bus: Crowded SITA buses (often blue or green-and-white) are most useful for traversing the popular Amalfi Coast; see "Getting Around the Amalfi Coast—By Bus" on page 107.

By Taxi: For €100, you can take a 30-mile taxi ride from Naples directly to your Sorrento hotel; agree on a set price without the meter and pay upon arrival. You can hire a cab on Capri for about €70/hour. Taxis in the Amalfi Coast are generally expensive, and more than willing to overcharge you, but they can be convenient, especially with a larger group. See "Getting Around the Amalfi Coast—By Taxi" on page 108.

By Boat: Several ferry companies service the Naples, Sorrento, and Amalfi Coast areas. While these can change from year to year, major companies include Caremar (www.caremar. it), SNAV (www.snav.it), Gescab (a.k.a. NLG Jet, www.gescab.it), Metrò del Mare (www.metrodelmare.net), Navigazione Libera del Golfo (www.navlib.it), and Alilauro (www.alilauro.it). Each company has different destinations and prices; some compete for the same trips. The quicker the trip, the higher the price. A hydrofoil, called a "jet boat," skims between Naples and Sorrento—it's faster, safer from pickpockets, more scenic, and more expensive than the train (6/day, more in summer, departs roughly every 2 hours starting at 9:00, 35 minutes, €12-13). A taxi from Naples' Centrale train station to its port costs about €12-15.

For schedules to Capri, you can check online (www.capri-tourism.com; click "Shipping Timetable"), at any TI, or at Naples' Molo Beverello boat dock. Ticket windows clearly display the next available departure. The number of boats that run per day depends on the season. Trips are canceled in bad weather. Most boats charge €2 or so for luggage.

If you plan to arrive at and leave a destination by boat, note the return times—the last boat usually leaves before 19:00.

tavola calda with hot ready-to-eat dishes (€3-4); and a tiny meat, cheese, and bread shop with all you need for a cheap meal to go. It offers honest pricing and simple, peaceful, air-conditioned indoor seating (no cover, open Mon-Sat 7:00-21:00, Sun 9:00-14:00, 3 blocks below museum at Via Conte di Ruvo 21, between Via Pessina and Via Bellini, tel. 081-549-9660).

Salumeria Pasquale Carrino is a tiny *salumi* shop with an exuberant owner—the fun-loving and flamboyant Pasquale—who turns sandwich-making into a show (€3-7 sandwiches good for two people, Mon-Sat 8:00-15:00 & 17:00-20:00, closed Sun, 100 yards from museum—walk to the northwest corner of the building and cross two crosswalks to Via Salvator Rosa 10, tel. 081-564-0889).

A Romantic Splurge on the Harbor

Ristorante la Scialuppa ("The Rowboat") is a great bet for a fine local meal on the harbor. Located in the romantic Santa Lucia district, you'll walk across the causeway to the Castel dell'Ovo in the fisherman's quarter (the castle on the island) just off Via Partenope. They boast fine indoor and outdoor seating, attentive waitstaff, a wonderful assortment of *antipasti*, great seafood, and predictably high prices (€10 pizza, €14 pastas, €18 *secondi,* reservations smart, Borgo Marinari 4, tel. 081-764-5333, www.lascialuppa.it).

Near the Station

While far from high cuisine, these functional options are worth considering if you're on the way back to catch your train, or if you're sleeping in this neighborhood and don't want to venture far: **La Cantina dei Mille,** a block in front of the train station, is a traditional family-style place serving good, basic Neapolitan food to good, basic Neapolitans (€5-7 pizza, pasta, and *secondi,* hefty service charge, daily 12:00-16:00 & 17:00-24:00; with your back to the station, it's about halfway up the left side of Piazza Garibaldi at #126; tel. 081-283-448). Next door, **Iris** is another decent choice. The recommended **Grand Hotel Europa** has a restaurant peacefully buried in its basement, offering friendly service and a fine value (€18 fixed-price dinners include water and coffee, dinner served 19:00-22:30).

Naples Connections

From Naples by Boat to: Sorrento (6/day, more in summer, departs roughly every 2 hours starting at 9:00, 35 minutes, €12-13), **Capri** (roughly 2/hour, 45 minutes, €19-21); for more information, see www.snav.it and www.navlib.it. Seasonal boats to **Positano** (summer only, 4/day, 1.25-1.5 hours, €17) continue on to **Amalfi** (1.5-2 hours, €18).

By Train to: Rome (at least hourly, 1.25 hours on Frecciarossa express trains, €45; otherwise 2 hours, €11-22), **Florence** (3/day direct, 3 hours, €72; otherwise about hourly with change in Rome, 4.25 hours, €56-59), **Salerno** (2/hour, 35-60 minutes, €7.50-17, change in Salerno for boats to Amalfi and Positano; avoid slower trains that leave from Garibaldi Station), **Paestum** (10/day, 1.5 hours, €7.50, tickets sold at ticket counter and tobacco shops but not from machines, direction: Sapri), **Brindisi** (8/day, 4.75-7 hours, overnight possible, €20-48 depending on speed; from Brindisi, ferries sail to Greece), **Milan** (direct trains hourly, 5 hours, €100, more frequent with change in Rome, overnight possible), **Venice** (almost hourly, 5.5-7 hours with changes in Bologna or Rome, €121, overnight possible), **Palermo** (2/day direct, 9-9.5 hours, €53, overnight possible), **Nice** (2/day, 12 hours with change in Genoa), **Paris** (3/day, 13-15 hours with change in Rome or Milan). Any train listed on the schedule as leaving Napoli PG or Napoli-Garibaldi departs not from Napoli Centrale, but from the adjacent Garibaldi Station.

Note that the departures listed above are Trenitalia connections; a private rail company called Italo offers additional options to **Rome, Salerno, Florence, Milan,** and **Venice.** While Italo may be cheaper (if you book long in advance), it doesn't accept railpasses (for details on Italo visit www.italotreno.it).

By Circumvesuviana Train: See the "Getting Around the Region" sidebar for information on getting to Herculaneum, Pompeii, and Sorrento.

To Pompeii: To visit the ancient site of Pompeii, don't use national train connections to the city of Pompei (which is far from the site). You're better off on the Circumvesuviana train, which takes you to the Pompei Scavi-Villa dei Misteri stop near the actual site.

POMPEII AND NEARBY

Pompeii • Herculaneum • Vesuvius

Stopped in their tracks by the eruption of Mount Vesuvius in A.D. 79, Pompeii and Herculaneum offer the best look anywhere at what life in Rome must have been like around 2,000 years ago. These two cities of well-preserved ruins are yours to explore. Of the two sites, Pompeii is grander, while Herculaneum is smaller and more intimate; both are easily reached from Naples on the Circumvesuviana commuter train. Vesuvius, still smoldering ominously, rises up on the horizon. It last erupted in 1944, and is still an active volcano. Buses from the train stations at Herculaneum or Pompeii drop you a steep half-hour hike from the summit.

Pompeii

A once-thriving commercial port of 20,000, Pompeii (worth ▲▲▲) grew from Greek and Etruscan roots to become an important Roman city. Then, on August 24, A.D. 79, everything changed. Vesuvius erupted and began to bury the city under 30 feet of hot volcanic ash. For the archaeologists who excavated it centuries later, this was a shake-and-bake windfall, teaching them volumes about daily Roman life. Pompeii was accidentally redis- covered in 1599; excavations began in 1748.

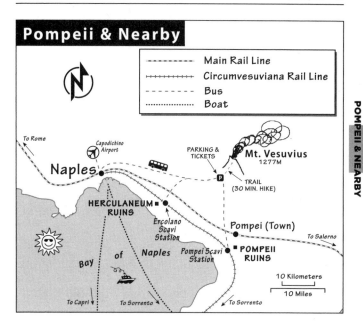

Pompeii & Nearby

Main Rail Line
Circumvesuviana Rail Line
Bus
Boat

To Rome

Capodichino Airport

PARKING & TICKETS

Mt. Vesuvius
1277M

Naples

TRAIL
(30 MIN. HIKE)

HERCULANEUM RUINS

Ercolano Scavi Station

Pompei (Town)

To Salerno

Bay of Naples

Pompei Scavi Station

POMPEII RUINS

10 Kilometers

10 Miles

To Capri

To Sorrento

To Sorrento

Orientation to Pompeii

Cost: €11, cash only; €20 combo-ticket includes Pompeii and three lesser sites (valid 3 consecutive days). Also consider the Campania ArteCard if visiting other sites in the region.

Hours: Daily April-Oct 8:30-19:30, Nov-March 8:30-17:00 (last entry 1.5 hours before closing).

Closures: Be warned that some buildings and streets are bound to be closed for restoration when you visit.

Crowd-Beating Tips: On busy days, there can be a line of up to 30 minutes to buy a ticket. If you anticipate lines, buy your ticket at the "info point" kiosk at the train station (same price as at the site, credit cards accepted).

Getting There: Pompeii is roughly midway between Naples and Sorrento on the Circumvesuviana train line (2/hour, €2.90 and 40 minutes from Naples, one-way, not covered by railpasses). Get off at the Pompei Scavi-Villa dei Misteri stop; from Naples, it's the stop after Torre Annunziata. The DD express trains (6/day) bypass several stations but do stop at Pompei Scavi, shaving 10 minutes off the trip from Naples. From the Pompei Scavi train station, it's just a two-minute walk to the Porta Marina entrance: Turn right and walk down the road about a block to the entrance (on your left).

Pompei vs. Pompei Scavi: Pompei is the name of a separate train station on the national rail network that's a long, dull walk

POMPEII & NEARBY

Pompeii

VILLA DEI MISTERI

VESUVIUS (IN DISTANCE)

To Naples

VIA SEPOLCRI

PORTA DI ERCOLANO

See Pompeii Tour map

PORTA DEL VESUVIO

PATH

CITY

HOUSE OF THE VETTII

HOUSE OF THE FAUN

VIA FORTUNA

BATHS OF THE FORUM

CAFETERIA & WC

FORUM

To Naples

A-3

AUTOSTRADA

CAMPING ZEUS OFFICE

CIRCUMVESUVIANA TRAIN STATION (WC & BAG STORAGE)

B Bus to Vesuvius

PORTA MARINA MAIN ENTRANCE

To Naples

SS-18

TICKETS

EXIT

TICKETS

Piazza Esedra

RISTORANTE SUISSE

HOTEL VITTORIA

VIA M.A.55.

200 Meters

200 Yards

A-3

To Salerno

To Sorrento

from the ruins. Make sure you're taking the Circumvesuviana commuter train to Pompei Scavi (*scavi* means "excavations").

Parking: Parking is available at Camping Zeus, next to the Pompei Scavi train station (€2.50/hour, €10/12 hours, 10 percent discount with this book); several other campgrounds/parking lots are nearby.

Information: The "info point" kiosk at the station is a private agency selling tours (not a real TI; see "Tours," later), but they can provide some information and also sell tickets for the site.

Be sure to pick up the free, helpful map at the entrance (ask for it when you buy your ticket, or check at the info window to the left of the WCs—the maps aren't available within the walls of Pompeii). Tel. 081-857-5347, www.pompeiisites.org.

The bookshop sells the small Pompeii and Herculaneum *Past and Present* book. Its plastic overlays allow you to re-create the ruins (€12; if you buy from a street vendor, pay no more than that).

Tours: My **self-guided tour** in this chapter covers the basics and provides a good framework for exploring the site on your own.

Guided tours leave every hour from the "info point" kiosk near the train station (€12). You can also sign up for a guided tour of Pompeii offered to Rick Steves readers through Naples-based Mondo Tours (€12, Mon-Fri at 10:00, meet at Ristorante Suisse, on Piazza Esedra, down the hill from the Porta Marina entrance).

Private guides (around €110/2 hours) of varying quality cluster near the ticket booth at the site and may try to herd you into a group with other travelers, which makes the price more reasonable for you. For a private two-hour tour, consider **Gaetano Manfredi,** who is pricey but brings energy and theatricality to his tours (€120 for up to 4 people, book in advance by email, www.pompeii tourguide.com, gaetanoguide@hotmail.it). **Antonio Somma** specializes in Pompeii (€120 for up to 8 people, price can vary with the season and number of people, book in advance, evening tel. 081-850-1992, daytime mobile 393-406-3824 or 339-891-9489, www.pompeitour.com, info@pompeitour.com). Antonio can organize transport for visitors who want to fill up the rest of the day with a trip to the Amalfi Coast. Parents, note that the ancient brothel and its sexually explicit frescoes are included on tours; let your guide know if you'd rather skip that stop.

Audioguides are available from a kiosk near the ticket booth at the Porta Marina entrance (€6.50, €10/2 people, ID required), but they offer basically the same info as your free booklet.

Length of This Tour: Allow two hours, or three if you visit the theater and amphitheater. With less time, focus on the Forum, Baths of the Forum, House of the Faun, and brothel.

Baggage Check: The train station offers luggage storage for €3/bag (by the WC). Or use the free baggage check near the turnstiles at the site entrance.

Services: There's a WC at the train station. The site has two WCs—one near the entrance and another in the cafeteria.

Eating: The Ciao cafeteria within the site serves good sandwiches, pizza, and pasta at a reasonable price. A few mediocre restaurants cluster between the entrance and the train station. Your cheapest bet may be to bring your own food for a discreet picnic.

Starring: Roofless (collapsed) but otherwise intact Roman buildings, plaster casts of hapless victims, a few erotic frescoes, and the dawning realization that these ancient people were not that different from us.

Background

Pompeii, founded in 600 B.C., eventually became a booming Roman trading city. Not rich, not poor, it was middle class—a perfect example of typical Roman life. Most streets would have been lined with stalls and jammed with customers from sunup to sundown. Chariots vied with shoppers for street space. Two

thousand years ago, Rome controlled the entire Mediterranean—making it a kind of free-trade zone—and Pompeii was a central and bustling port.

There were no posh neighborhoods in Pompeii. Rich and poor mixed it up as elegant houses existed side by side with simple homes. While nearby Herculaneum would have been a classier place to live (traffic-free streets, fancier houses, far better drainage), Pompeii was the place for action and shopping. It served an estimated 20,000 residents with more than 40 bakeries, 30 brothels, and 130 bars, restaurants, and hotels. With most of its buildings covered by brilliant white ground-marble stucco, Pompeii in A.D. 79 was an impressive town.

As you tour Pompeii, remember that its best art is in the Archaeological Museum in Naples (described in the previous chapter).

Self-Guided Tour

• *Just past the ticket-taker, start your approach up to the...*

❶ Porta Marina

The city of Pompeii was born on the hill ahead of you. This was the original town gate. Before Vesuvius blew and filled in the

harbor, the sea came nearly to here. Notice the two openings in the gate (ahead, up the ramp). Both were left open by day to admit major traffic. At night, the larger one was closed for better security.

• *Pass through the Porta Marina and continue up to the top of the* street, pausing at the three large stepping-stones in the middle.

❷ Pompeii's Streets

Every day, Pompeiians flooded the streets with gushing water to clean them. These stepping-stones let pedestrians cross without getting their sandals wet. Chariots traveling in either direction could straddle the stones (all had standard-size axles). A single

stepping-stone in a road means it was a one-way street, a pair indicates an ordinary two-way, and three (like this) signifies a major thoroughfare. The basalt stones are the original Roman pavement. The sidewalks (elevated to hide the plumbing) were paved with bits of broken pots (an ancient form of recy-

cling) and studded with reflective bits of white marble. These "cats' eyes" helped people get around after dark, either by moonlight or with the help of lamps.

• *Continue straight ahead, don your mental toga, and enter the city as*

*the Romans once did. The road opens up into the spacious main square:
the Forum. Stand at the near end of this rectangular space and look toward Mount Vesuvius.*

❸ The Forum (Foro)

Pompeii's commercial, religious, and political center stands at the
intersection of the city's two main streets. While it's the most ruined part of Pompeii, it's grand nonetheless. Picture the piazza
surrounded by two-story buildings
on all sides. The pedestals that line
the square once held statues (now
safely displayed in the museum in
Naples). In its heyday, Pompeii's
citizens gathered here in the main
square to shop, talk politics, and
socialize. Business took place in
the important buildings that lined
the piazza.

The Forum was dominated by the **Temple of Jupiter,** at the far
end (marked by a half-dozen ruined columns atop a stair-step base).
Jupiter was the supreme god of the Roman pantheon—you might
be able to make out his little white marble head at the center-rear
of the temple.

At the near end of the Forum (behind where you're standing)
is the **curia,** or city hall. Like many Roman buildings, it was built
with brick and mortar, then covered with marble walls and floors.
To your left (as you face Vesuvius and the Temple of Jupiter) is the
basilica, or courthouse.

Since Pompeii was a pretty typical Roman town, it has the
same layout and components that you'll find in any Roman city—
main square, curia, basilica, temples, axis of roads, and so on. All
power converged at the Forum: religious (the temple), political (the
curia), judicial (the basilica), and commercial (this piazza was the
main marketplace). Even the power of the people was expressed
here, since this is where they gathered to vote. Imagine the hubbub
of this town square in its heyday.

Look beyond the Temple of Jupiter. Five miles to the north
looms the ominous backstory to this site: **Mount Vesuvius.** Mentally draw a triangle up from the two remaining peaks to recon-
struct the mountain before the eruption. When it blew, Pompeiians had no idea that they were living under a volcano, as Vesuvius
hadn't erupted for 1,200 years. Imagine the wonder—then the
horror—as a column of pulverized rock roared upward, and then
ash began to fall. The weight of the ash and small rocks collapsed
Pompeii's roofs later that day, crushing people who had taken refuge inside buildings instead of fleeing the city.

Pompeii Tour

VESUVIUS (IN DISTANCE)

PATH

CITY WALLS

PORTA DEL VESUVIO

UNEXCAVATED AREA

HOUSE OF THE VETTII (MAY BE CLOSED) ⑬

VIC. VETTII

VIA VESUVIO

VIA NOLA

HOUSE OF THE FAUN

⑫

PORTA DI ERCOLANO

VIA MERCURIO

⑪

TABERNA HEDONES

⑧

VIA CONSULARE

⑨ ⑩

VIA FORTUNA

VIA STABIANA

⑭

CITY WALLS

VIA

⑦

VIA AUGUSTALI

⑮

CAFETERIA & **WC**

⑥

VIA TEATRI

VIA ABBONDANZA

To ⑱

TEMPLE OF JUPITER

FORUM

③ ⑤

THEATER

⑯

TEATRO PICCOLO

PORTA MARINA ENTRANCE

① ②

④

⑰

TICKETS

WALK ENDS

CIRCUM-VESUVIANA TRAIN STATION

👣 **WALK BEGINS**

EXIT

CITY WALLS

VIA DEI TEATRI

PIAZZA ESEDRA ENTRANCE

Piazza Esedra

TICKETS

RISTORANTE SUISSE

HOTEL VITTORIA

SS-18

VIA PLINIO

200 Meters

200 Yards

① Porta Marina
② Pompeii's Streets
③ Forum
④ Basilica
⑤ Via Abbondanza
⑥ Fish & Produce Market; Plaster Casts of Victims
⑦ Baths of the Forum
⑧ Fast-Food Joint
⑨ House of the Tragic Poet
⑩ Aqueduct Arch
⑪ House of the Faun
⑫ Original Lead Pipes
⑬ House of the Vettii
⑭ Bakery & Mill
⑮ Brothel
⑯ Temple of Isis
⑰ Theater & Piccolo Theater
⑱ To Amphitheater

POMPEII & NEARBY

• *As you face Vesuvius, the basilica is to your left, lined with stumps of columns. Step inside and see the layout.*

❹ Basilica

Pompeii's basilica was a first-century palace of justice. This ancient law court has the same floor plan later adopted by many Christian churches (which are also called basilicas). The big central hall (or nave) is flanked by rows of columns marking off narrower side aisles. Along the side walls are traces of the original marble.

The columns—now stumps all about the same height—were not ruined by the volcano. Rather, they were left unfinished when Vesuvius blew. Pompeii had been devastated by an earthquake in A.D. 62, and was just in the process of rebuilding the basilica when Vesuvius erupted, 17 years later. The half-built columns show off the technology of the day. Uniform bricks were stacked around a cylindrical core. Once finished, they would have been coated with marble dust stucco to simulate marble columns—an economical construction method found throughout Pompeii (and the Roman Empire).

Besides the earthquake and the eruption, Pompeii's buildings have suffered other ravages over the years, including Spanish plunderers (c. 1800), 19th-century souvenir hunters, WWII bombs, wild vegetation, another earthquake in 1980, and modern neglect. The fact that the entire city was covered by the eruption of A.D. 79 actually helped preserve it, saving it from the sixth-century barbarians who plundered many other towns into oblivion.

• *Exit the basilica and cross the short side of the square, where the city's main street hits the Forum.*

❺ Via Abbondanza

Glance down Via Abbondanza, Pompeii's main street. Lined with shops, bars, and restaurants, it was a lively, pedestrian-only zone. The three "beaver-teeth" stones are traffic barriers that kept chariots out. On the corner (just to the left), take a close look at the dark travertine column standing next to the white one. Notice that the marble drums of the white column are not chiseled entirely round—another construction project left unfinished when Vesuvius erupted.

• *Head toward Vesuvius, walking along the right side of the Forum. Immediately to the right of the Temple of Jupiter (just before the four round arches), a door leads into the market hall, where you'll find two glass cases.*

❻ Fish and Produce Market— Plaster Casts of Victims

As the frescoes on the wall (just inside on the left) indicate, this is where Pompeiians came to buy their food—fish, bread, chickens, and so on. These fine examples of Roman art—with their glimpses of everyday life and their mastery of depth and illusion—would not be matched until the Renaissance, a thousand years after the fall of Rome.

The glass cases hold casts of Pompeiians, eerily captured in their last moments. They were quickly suffocated by a superheated avalanche of gas and ash, and their bodies were encased in volcanic debris. While excavating, modern archaeologists detected hollow spaces underfoot, created when the victims' bodies decomposed. By gently filling the holes with plaster, the archaeologists were able to create molds of the Pompeiians who were caught in the disaster.

• *Continue on, leaving the Forum through an arch behind the Temple of Jupiter. Here you'll find a pedestrian-only road sign (ahead on the right corner, above the* REG VII INS IV *sign) and more "beaver-teeth" traffic blocks. The modern cafeteria is the only eatery inside the archaeological site (with a coffee bar and WC upstairs). Twenty yards past the cafeteria, on the left-hand side at #24, is the entrance to the...*

❼ Baths of the Forum (Terme del Foro)

Pompeii had six public baths, each with a men's and a women's section. You're in the men's zone. The leafy courtyard at the entrance was the gymnasium. After working out, clients could relax with a hot bath *(caldarium),* warm bath *(tepidarium),* or cold plunge *(frigidarium).*

The first big, plain room you enter served as the **dressing room.** Holes on the walls were for pegs to hang clothing. High up, the window (with a faded Neptune underneath) was originally covered with a less-translucent Roman glass. Walk over the non-slip mosaics into the next room.

The *tepidarium* is ringed by mini-statues or *telamones* (male caryatids, figures used as supporting pillars), which divided the lockers. Clients would undress and warm up here, perhaps stretching out on one of the bronze benches near the bronze heater for a massage. Look at the ceiling—half crushed by the

The Eruption of Vesuvius

At about 1:00 in the afternoon on August 24, A.D. 79, Mount Vesuvius erupted, sending a mushroom cloud of ash, dust, and rocks 12 miles into the air. It spewed for 18 hours straight, as winds blew the cloud southward. The white-gray ash settled like a heavy snow on Pompeii, its weight eventually collapsing roofs and floors, but leaving the walls intact. And though most of Pompeii's 20,000 residents fled that day, about 2,000 stayed behind.

Although the city of Herculaneum was closer to the volcano—about four miles away—at first it largely escaped the rain of ash, due to the direction of the wind. However, 12 hours after Vesuvius awoke, the type of eruption suddenly changed. The mountain let loose a superheated avalanche of ash, pumice, and gas. This red-hot "pyroclastic flow" sped down the side of the mountain at nearly 100 miles per hour, engulfing Herculaneum and cooking its residents alive. Several more flows over the next few hours further entombed Herculaneum, burying it in nearly 60 feet of hot material that later cooled into rock, freezing the city in time. Then, at around 7:30 in the morning, another pyroclastic flow headed south and struck Pompeii, dealing a fatal blow to those who'd remained behind.

eruption and half intact, with its fine blue-and-white stucco work.

Next, admire the engineering in the steam-bath room, or *caldarium.* The double floor was heated from below—so nice with bare feet (look into the grate to see the brick support towers). The double walls with brown terra-cotta tiles held the heat. Romans soaked in the big tub, which was filled with hot water. Opposite the big tub is a fountain, which spouted water onto the hot floor, creating steam. The lettering on the fountain reminded those enjoying the room which two politicians paid for it...and how much it cost them (5,250 *sestertii*). To keep condensation from dripping annoyingly from the ceiling, fluting (ribbing) was added to carry water down the walls.

• *Today's visitors exit the baths through the original entry. If you're a bit hungry, immediately across the street is an ancient...*

❽ Fast-Food Joint

After a bath, it was only natural to want a little snack. So, just across the street is a fast-food joint, marked by a series of rectangular marble counters. Most ancient Romans didn't cook for themselves in their tiny apartments, so to-go places like this were commonplace. The holes in the counters held the pots for food. Each container was like a thermos, with a wooden lid to keep the soup hot, the wine cool, and so on. Notice the groove in the front doorstep and the holes out on the curb. The holes likely accommodated cords for stretching awnings over the sidewalk to shield the clientele from the hot sun, while the grooves were for the shop's folding accordion doors. Look at the wheel grooves in the pavement, worn down through centuries of use. Nearby are more stepping-stones for pedestrians to cross the flooded streets.

• *Just a few steps uphill from the fast-food joint, at #5 (with a locked gate), is the...*

➒ House of the Tragic Poet (Casa del Poeta Tragico)

This house is typical Roman style. The entry is flanked by two family-owned shops (each with a track for a collapsing accordion door). The home is like a train running straight away from the street: atrium (with skylight and pool to catch the rain), den (where deals were made by the shopkeeper), and garden (with rooms facing it and a shrine to remember both the gods and family ancestors). In the entryway is the famous "Beware of Dog" *(Cave Canem)* mosaic.

Today's visitors enter the home by the back door (circle around to the left). On your way there, look for the modern exposed pipe on the left side of the lane; this is the same as ones used in the ancient plumbing system, hidden beneath the raised sidewalk. Inside the house, the grooves on the marble well-head in the entry hall (possibly closed) were formed by generations of inhabitants dragging the bucket up by rope. The richly frescoed dining room is off the garden. Diners lounged on their couches (the Roman custom) and enjoyed frescoes with fake "windows," giving the illusion of a bigger and airier room. Next to the dining room is a humble BBQ-style kitchen with a little closet for the toilet (the kitchen and bathroom shared the same plumbing).

• *Return to the fast-food place and continue about 10 yards downhill to the big intersection. From the center of the intersection, look left to see a giant arch, framing a nice view of Mount Vesuvius.*

➓ Aqueduct Arch—Running Water

Water was critical for this city of 20,000 people, and this arch was part of Pompeii's water-delivery system. A 100-mile-long aqueduct carried fresh water down from the hillsides to a big reservoir perched at the highest point of the city wall. Since overall water pressure was disappointing, Pompeiians built arches like the brick one you see here (originally covered in marble) with hidden water tanks at the top. Located just below the altitude of the main tank, these smaller tanks were filled by gravity and provided each neighborhood with reliable pressure.

• *If you're thirsty, fill your water bottle from the modern fountain. Then continue straight downhill one block (50 yards) to #2 on the left.*

⓫ House of the Faun (Casa del Fauno)

Stand across the street and marvel at the grand entry with *"HAVE"* (hail to you) as a welcome mat. Go in. Notice the two shrines above the entryway—one dedicated to the gods, the other to this wealthy family's ancestors.

You are standing in Pompeii's largest home, where you're greeted by the delightful small bronze statue of the *Dancing Faun,* famed for its realistic movement and fine proportion. (The original is in Naples' Archaeological Museum.) With 40 rooms and 27,000 square feet, the House of the Faun covers an entire city block. The next floor mosaic, with an intricate diamond-like design, decorates the homeowner's office. Beyond that is the famous floor mosaic of the *Battle of Alexander.* (The original is also at the museum in Naples.) In 333 B.C., Alexander the Great beat Darius and the Persians. Romans had great respect for Alexander, the first great emperor before Rome's. While most of Pompeii's nouveau riche had notoriously bad taste and stuffed their palaces with over-the-top, mismatched decor, this guy had class. Both the faun (an ancient copy of a famous Greek statue) and the Alexander mosaic show an appreciation for history.

The house's back courtyard leads to the exit in the far-right corner. It's lined with pillars rebuilt after the A.D. 62 earthquake. Take a close look at the brick, mortar, and fake marble stucco veneer.

• *Sneak out of the House of the Faun through its back door and turn right. (If this exit is closed, return to the entrance and make a U-turn left, around to the back of the house.) Thirty yards down, along the right-hand side of the street are metal cages protecting...*

⓬ Original Lead Pipes

These 2,000-year-old pipes (made of lead imported from Britannia) were part of the city's elaborate water system. From the aqueduct-fed water tank at the high end of town, three independent pipe systems supplied water to the city: one for baths, one for private homes, and one for public water fountains. If there was a water shortage, democratic priorities prevailed: First the baths were cut off, then the private homes. The last water supply to go was the public fountains, where all citizens could get drinking and cooking water.

• *If the street's not closed off, take your first left (on Vicolo dei Vettii), walk about 20 yards, and find the entrance (on the left) to the next stop. (If the street is closed, turn right down the street marked REG VI INS XIV and skip down to the next set of directions.)*

⑱ House of the Vettii (Casa dei Vettii)

Pompeii's best-preserved home has been completely blocked off for years; unfortunately, it's unlikely to reopen in time for your visit. The House of the Vettii was the bachelor pad of two wealthy merchant brothers. If you can see the entryway, you may spot the huge erection. This is not pornography. There's a meaning here: The penis and the sack of money balance each other on the goldsmith scale above a fine bowl of fruit. Translation: Only with a balance of fertility and money can you have abundance.

If it's open, step into the atrium with its ceiling open to the sky to collect light and rainwater. The pool, while decorative, was a functional water-supply tank. It's flanked by large money boxes anchored to the floor. The brothers were certainly successful merchants, and possibly moneylenders, too.

Exit on the right, passing the tight servant quarters, and go into the kitchen, with its bronze cooking pots (and an exposed lead pipe on the back wall). The passage dead-ends in the little Venus Room, which features erotic frescoes behind glass.

Return to the atrium and pass into the big colonnaded garden. It was replanted according to the plan indicated by the traces of roots that were excavated from the volcanic ash. Richly frescoed entertainment rooms ring this courtyard. Circle counterclockwise. The dining room is finely decorated in black and "Pompeiian red" (from iron rust). Study the detail. Notice the lead humidity seal between the wall and the floor, designed to keep the moisture-sensitive frescoes dry. (Had Leonardo da Vinci taken this clever step, his *Last Supper* in Milan might be in better shape today.) Continuing around, you'll see more of the square white stones inlaid in the floor. Imagine them reflecting like cats' eyes as the brothers and their friends wandered around by oil lamp late at night. Frescoes in the Yellow Room (near the exit) show off the ancient mastery of perspective, which would not be matched elsewhere in Europe for nearly 1,500 years.

• *Facing the entrance to the House of the Vettii, turn left and walk downhill one long block (along Vicolo dei Vettii) to a T-intersection (Via della Fortuna), marked by a stone fountain with a bull's head for a spout. Intersections like this were busy neighborhood centers, where the rent was highest and people gathered. With the fountain at your back, turn left, then immediately right, walking along a gently curving road (Vicolo Storto). On the left side of the street, at #22, find four big stone cylinders.*

⑭ Bakery and Mill (Forno e Mulini)

The brick oven looks like a modern-day pizza oven. The stubby stone towers are flour grinders. Grain was poured into the top, and donkeys or slaves pushed wood-en bars that turned the stones. The powdered grain dropped out of the bottom as flour—flavored with tiny bits of rock. Each neighborhood had a bakery like this.

Continue to the next intersection (Via degli Augustali, where there's another fast-food joint, at #32) and turn left. As you walk, look at the destructive power of all the vines, and notice how deeply the chariot grooves have worn into the pavement. Deep grooves could break wagon wheels. The suddenly ungroovy stretch indicates that this road was in the process of being repaved when the eruption shut everything down.

• *Head about 50 yards down this (obviously one-way) street to #44 (on the left). Here you'll find the Taberna Hedones (with a small atrium, den, and garden). This bar still has its original floor and, deeper in, the mosaic arch of a grotto fountain. Just past the tavern, turn right and walk downhill to #18, on the right.*

Possible detour: If the road past the tavern is blocked off, here's another way to reach the next stop: First, backtrack to the Forum—go back the way you came, turn left at the bull's-head fountain, then turn left again at the aqueduct arch. Back in the Forum, head down to the far end and turn left onto the main street, Via dell'Abbondanza (which we looked down earlier—remember the beaver teeth?). Follow this, turning left up the second street (after the fountain, marked REG VII INS I, *with a small* Vicolo del Lupanare *sign). This leads to the entrance of the...*

⑮ Brothel (Lupanare)

You'll find the biggest crowds in Pompeii at a place that was likely popular 2,000 ago, too—the brothel. Prostitutes were nicknamed *lupe* (she-wolves), alluding to the call they made when trying to attract business. The brothel was a simple place, with beds and pillows made of stone. The ancient graffiti includes tallies and exotic names of the women, indicating the prostitutes came from all corners of the Mediterranean (it also served as feedback from satisfied customers). The faded frescoes above the cells may have been a kind of menu for services offered. Note the idealized women (white, which was considered beautiful; one wears an early bra) and the rougher men (dark, considered horny). The bed legs came with little disk-like barriers to keep critters from crawling up.

• *Leaving the brothel, go right, then take the first left, and continue going downhill two blocks to the intersection with Pompeii's main drag, Via dell'Abbondanza. The Forum—and exit—are to the right, for those who may wish to opt out from here.*

The huge amphitheater—which is certainly skippable—is 10 minutes to your left. But for now, go left for 60 yards, then turn right just beyond the fountain, and walk down Via dei Teatri. Turn left before the columns, and head downhill another 60 yards to #28, which marks the...

⑯ Temple of Isis

This Egyptian temple served Pompeii's Egyptian community. The little white stucco shrine with the modern plastic roof housed holy water from the Nile. Isis, from Egyptian myth, was one of many foreign gods adopted by the eclectic Romans. Pompeii must have had a synagogue, too, but it has yet to be excavated.

• *Exit the temple where you entered, and go right. At the next intersection, turn right again, and head downhill to the adjacent theaters. Your goal is the large theater down the corridor at #20, but if it's closed, look at the smaller but similar theater (Teatro Piccolo) just beyond at #19.*

⑰ Theater

Originally a Greek theater (Greeks built theirs with the help of a hillside), this was the birthplace of the Greek port here in 470 B.C. During Roman times, the theater sat 5,000 people in three sets of seats, all with different prices: the five marble terraces up close (filled with romantic wooden seats for two), the main section, and the cheap nosebleed section (surviving only on the high end, near the trees). The square stones above the cheap seats once supported a canvas rooftop. Take note of the high-profile boxes, flanking the stage, for guests of honor. From this perch, you can see the gladiator barracks—the colonnaded courtyard beyond the theater. They lived in tiny rooms, trained in the courtyard, and fought in the nearby amphitheater.

• *You've seen Pompeii's highlights. When you're ready to leave, backtrack to the main road and turn left, going uphill to the Forum, where you'll find the main entrance/exit.*

However, there's much more to see—three-quarters of Pompeii's 164 acres have been excavated, but this tour has covered only a third of the site. After the theater—if you still have energy to see more—go back to the main road and take a right toward the eastern part of the site, where the crowds thin out. Go straight for about 10 minutes, likely jogging right after a bit (just follow the posted maps). You'll wind up passing through a pretty, forested area. At the far end is the...

⓲ Amphitheater

If you can, climb to the upper level of the amphitheater (though the stairs are often blocked). With Vesuvius looming in the back-

ground, mentally replace the tourists below with gladiators and wild animals locked in combat. Walk along the top of the amphitheater and look down into the grassy rectangular area surrounded by columns. This is the **Palaestra,** an area once used for athletic training. (If you can't get to the top of the amphitheater, you can see the Palaestra from outside—in fact, you can't miss it, as it's right next door.) Facing the other way, look for the bell tower that tops the roofline of the modern city of Pompei, where locals go about their daily lives in the shadow of the volcano, just as their ancestors did 2,000 years ago.

• *If it's too crowded to bear hiking back along uneven lanes to the entrance, you can slip out the site's "back door," which is next to the amphitheater. Exiting, turn right and follow the site's wall all the way back to the entrance.*

Herculaneum

Smaller, less crowded, and not as ruined as its famous big sister, Herculaneum (worth ▲▲, "Ercolano" in Italian) offers a closer, more intimate peek into ancient Roman life but lacks the grandeur of Pompeii (there's barely a colonnade).

Orientation to Herculaneum

Cost and Hours: €11, €20 combo-ticket includes Pompeii and three lesser sites (valid 3 consecutive days); also covered by the Campania ArteCard. Open daily April-Oct 8:30-19:30, Nov-March 8:30-17:00, ticket office closes 1.5 hours earlier.

Getting There: Ercolano Scavi, the nearest train station to Herculaneum, is about 20 minutes from Naples and 50 minutes from Sorrento on the same Circumvesuviana train that goes to Pompeii. Walking from the Ercolano Scavi train station to the ruins takes 10 minutes: Leave the station and turn right, then left down the main drag; go eight blocks straight downhill to the end of the road, where you'll see the entrance to the ruins marked by a grand arch. (Skip Museo MAV.) Pass through the arch and continue 200 yards down the path to the ticket office in the modern building, taking in the bird's-eye first impression of the site to your right.

Information: Pick up a free, detailed map and excellent booklet at the info desk next to the ticket window. The booklet gives you a quick explanation of each building, keyed to the same numbers as the audioguides. (I've included some of these numbers in my self-guided tour, below.) There's a bookstore inside the site, next to the audioguide stand. Tel. 081-777-7008, www.pompeiisites.org.

Audioguide: The informative and interesting audioguide sheds light on the ruins and life in Herculaneum in the first century A.D. (€6.50, €10/2 people, ID required, cheaper version available for kids ages 4-10, pick up 100 yards after the ticket turnstiles, uses same numbers as info booklet).

Length of This Tour: Allow one hour.

Baggage Storage: Herculaneum is harder than Pompeii for those with luggage, but not impossible. Herculaneum's train station has lots of stairs and no baggage storage, but you can roll wheeled luggage down to the ruins and store it for free in a locked area in the ticket office building (pick up bags at least 30 minutes prior to site closing). To get back to the station, consider splurging on a €5 taxi (ask the staff to call one for you).

Services: There's a free WC in the ticket office building.

Eating: The site doesn't have a café of its own, but there are several eateries on the way from the train station.

Self-Guided Tour

Caked and baked by the same A.D. 79 eruption that pummeled Pompeii, Herculaneum is a small community of intact buildings with plenty of surviving detail. While Pompeii was initially smothered in ash, Herculaneum was spared at first—due to the direction of the wind—but got slammed about 12 hours after the eruption started by a superheated avalanche of ash and hot gases roaring off the volcano. The city was eventually buried under nearly 60 feet of ash, which hardened into tuff, perfectly preserving the city until excavations began in 1748.

After leaving the ticket building, go through the turnstiles and walk the path below the site to the entrance. Look seawards and note where the shoreline is today; before the eruption, it was just where you are standing, a quarter-mile inland. This gives you a sense of just how much volcanic material piled up. The present-day city of Ercolano looms just above the ruins. The modern buildings don't look much different from their ancient counterparts.

As you cross the modern bridge into the excavation site, look down into the moat-like ditch. On one side, you see Herculaneum's seafront wall. On the other, the wall that you've just been walking on is the solidifed ash layer from the volcano and shows how deeply the town was buried.

After crossing the bridge, stroll straight to the end of the street and find the **Seat of the Augustali** (Sede degli Augustali, #24). Decorated with frescoes of Hercules (for whom this city was named), it belonged to an association of freed slaves working together to climb their way up the ladder of Roman society. Here and farther on, look around doorways and ceilings to spot ancient wood charred by the pyroclastic flows. Most buildings were made of stone, with wooden floors and beams (which were preserved here by the ash but rarely survive at ancient sites).

Leave the building through the back and go to the right, down the lane. The adjacent *thermopolium* (#22) was the Roman equivalent of a lunch counter or fast-food joint, with giant jars for wine, oil, and snacks. Most of the buildings along here were shops, with apartments above.

A few steps on, the **Bottega ad Cucumas** wine shop (#19) still has charred remains of beams, and its drink list remains frescoed on the outside wall (under glass).

Take the next right, go halfway down the street, and on the left find the **House of Neptune and Amphitrite** (Casa di Nettuno e Anfitrite, #29). Outside, notice the intact upper floor and imagine it going even higher. Inside, you'll see colorful mosaics and a unique "frame" made of shells.

Back outside, continue downhill to the intersection, then head left for a block and go straight across the street into the don't-miss-it **sports complex** (*palestra;* #12). First you'll see a row of "marble" columns, which (look closer) are actually made of rounded bricks covered with a thick layer of plaster, shaped to look like carved marble. While important buildings in Rome had solid marble columns, these fakes are typical of ordinary buildings.

Look for the hole in the hillside and walk through one of the triangular-shaped entrances to find the highlight: the Hydra of Lerna, a sculpted bronze fountain that features the seven-headed monster defeated by Hercules as one of his 12 labors. If this cavernous space is unlit, go to the second doorway on the left wall and press the light switch.

Go back out to the street and downhill to the **House of the Deer** (Casa dei Cervi, #8). It's named for the statues of deer being attacked by dogs in the garden courtyard (these are copies; the originals are in the Archaeological Museum in Naples). As you wander through the rooms, notice the colorfully frescoed walls. Ancient Herculaneum, like all Roman cities of that age, was filled with color, rather than the stark white we often imagine (even the statues were painted).

Continue downhill through the archway. The **baths** (Terme Suburbane, #3; enter near the side of the statue, sometimes closed) illustrate the city's devastation. After you descend into the baths, look back at the steps. You'll see the original wood charred in the disaster, protected by the wooden planks you just walked on. At the bottom of the stairs, in the waiting room to the right, notice where the floor collapsed under the sheer weight of the volcanic debris. (The sunken pavement reveals the baths' heating system: hot air generated by wood-burning furnaces and circulated between the different levels of the floor.) A doorway in front of the stairs is still filled with solidified ash. Despite the damage, elements of refinement remain intact, such as the delicate stuccoes in the *caldarium* (hot bath).

Back outside, make your way down the steps to the sunken area just below. As you descend, you're walking across what was formerly Herculaneum's beach. Looking back, you'll see **arches** that were part of boat storage areas. Archaeologists used to wonder why so few victims were found in Herculaneum. But during

POMPEII & NEARBY

excavations in 1981, hundreds of skeletons were discovered here, between the wall of volcanic stone behind you and the city in front of you. Some of Herculaneum's 4,000 citizens tried to escape by sea, but were overtaken by the pyroclastic flows.

Thankfully, your escape is easier. Either follow the sounds of the water and continue through the tunnel; or, more scenically, backtrack and exit the same way you entered.

Vesuvius

The 4,000-foot-high Vesuvius, mainland Europe's only active volcano, has been sleeping restlessly since 1944. While Europe has

other dangerous volcanoes, only Vesuvius sits in the middle of a three-million-person metropolitan area that would be impossible to evacuate quickly. Many tourists don't know that you can easily visit the summit. Up top, it's desolate and lunarlike, and the rocks are newly created. Walk the entire accessible part of the crater lip for the most interesting views; the far end overlooks Pompeii. Be still. Listen to the wind and the occasional cascades of rocks tumbling into the crater. Any steam? Vesuvius is closed to visitors when erupting.

You can reach the volcano by bus, taxi, or private car (described below). No matter how you travel up, you'll land at the parking lot. From here it's a steep 30-minute hike (with a 950-foot elevation gain) to the top for a sweeping view of the Bay of Naples. Bring a coat; it's often cold and windy (especially Oct-April).

Cost and Hours: €10 covers entry to the national park (and a mandatory but brief introduction from a park guide, who then sets you free), daily April-Oct 9:30-17:00, until 18:00 in summer, Nov-March 9:30-15:00, last entry 1.5 hours before closing, no WC, tel. 081-865-3911 or 081-239-5653, www.parconazionaledelvesuvio.it.

Getting to Vesuvius

By Car or Taxi: Just drive to the end of the road and pay €2.50 to park. A taxi costs €90 round-trip from Naples, including a 2-hour wait; it's cheaper from Pompeii.

By Bus from Pompeii: From the Pompei Scavi train station on the Circumvesuviana line (just outside the main entrance to the Pompeii ruins), you have two bus services to choose from, each taking about three hours (40 minutes up, 40 minutes down, and about 1.5 hours at the summit).

Busvia del Vesuvio winds you up a bumpy private road through the back of the national park in a cross between a shuttle bus and a monster truck. It's a fun, more scenic way to go, but not for the easily queasy (€22 includes summit admission, runs hourly April-Oct daily 9:00-15:00, also at 16:00 and 17:00 June-Aug, rarely runs Nov-March—call for schedule, buy tickets at "info point" at Pompei Scavi train station, mobile 340-935-2616, www. busviadelvesuvio.com).

The old-fashioned **Vesuvius Trolley Tram** (Tramvia del Vesuvio) uses the main road up (€12 round-trip plus €10 summit admission, 10 percent discount with this book, 6/day, tickets sold at and departs from Camping Zeus next to Pompei Scavi train station, tel. 081-861-5320, www.campingzeus.it).

By Bus from Herculaneum: The quickest trip up is on the **Vesuvio Express.** These small buses leave from the Ercolano Scavi train station (on the Circumvesuviana line, where you get off for the Herculaneum ruins; €10 round-trip plus €10 summit admission, daily from 9:00, runs every 45 minutes based on demand, 20 minutes each way—about 2.5 hours total, office on square in front of train station, tel. 081-739-3666, www.vesuvioexpress.it).

SORRENTO AND CAPRI

Just an hour south of Naples and without a hint of big-city chaos, serene Sorrento makes an ideal home base for exploring this fascinating region, from Naples to the Amalfi Coast to Paestum. And the jet-setting island of Capri is just a short cruise from Sorrento, offering more charm and fun (outside of the crowded months of July and August) than its glitzy reputation would lead you to believe.

Sorrento

Wedged on a ledge under the mountains and over the Mediterranean, spritzed by lemon and olive groves, Sorrento is an attractive resort of 20,000 residents and, in summer, just as many tourists. It's as well-located for regional sightseeing as it is a fine place to stay and stroll. The Sorrentines have gone out of their way to create a completely safe and relaxed place for tourists to come and spend money. As 90 percent of the town's economy is tourism, everyone seems to speak fluent English and work for the Chamber of Commerce. This gateway to the Amalfi Coast has an unspoiled old quarter, a lively main shopping street, and a spectacular cliffside setting. Residents are proud of the many world-class romantics who've vacationed here, such as the famed tenor Enrico Caruso, who chose Sorrento as the place to spend his last weeks in 1921.

Sorrento Area & Capri

Bay of Naples

6 Kilometers

4 Miles

To Pompeii & Naples

Castellammare di Stabia

To Naples

S-145

Vico Equense

CIRCUMVESUVIANA RAIL LINE

Punta del Capo

Meta

To Amalfi

Positano

Sorrento

S-145

S-163

Massa Lubrense

Sant' Agata

Amalfi Coast

To Amalfi

Termini

Marina del Cantone

Galli Islands

Marina Grande

Blue Grotto

VILLA JOVIS

Anacapri

Capri

Capri Town

Gulf of Salerno

See detail map

SORRENTO & CAPRI

Planning Your Time

Sorrento itself has no world-class sights, but can easily give you a few pleasant hours. More importantly, Sorrento is a fine base for visiting Naples (by boat or train); Pompeii, Herculaneum, and Mount Vesuvius (by train, plus a bus for Vesuvius); the Amalfi Coast (by bus); and the island of Capri (by boat). All of these destinations are within an hour or so of Sorrento. Of the region's attractions, only Paestum's Greek temples are a little hard to reach from Sorrento, and even they can be seen in a long day.

Sorrento hibernates in winter, and many places close down from November through February or March.

Orientation to Sorrento

Downtown Sorrento is long and narrow. Piazza Tasso marks the town's center. The main drag, Corso Italia, runs parallel to the

sea, passing 50 yards below the train station, through Piazza Tasso, and then out toward the cape, where the road's name becomes Via Capo. Nearly everything mentioned here (except Meta beach and the hotels on Via Capo) is within a 10-minute walk of the station. The town is perched on a cliff (some hotels have elevators down to sundecks on the water); the best real beaches are a couple of miles away.

Sorrento has two different port areas: The Marina Piccola, below Piazza Tasso, is a functional harbor with boats to Naples and Capri, as well as cruise-ship tenders. (While the big cruise ships dock in Naples, smaller ships drop anchor at Sorrento.) The Marina Grande, below the other end of downtown, is like a little fishing village, with recommended restaurants and more charm.

Tourist Information

The helpful TI (labeled *Soggiorno e Turismo*)—located inside the Foreigners' Club—hands out the free monthly *Surrentum* magazine, with a great city map and schedules of boats, buses, concerts, and festivals (Mon-Fri 8:30-19:00, Sat 9:00-13:00, Sun 9:00-13:00 except closed Sun Oct-May; Via Luigi de Maio 35, tel. 081-807-4033, www.sorrentotourism.com; Nino, Fabiola, and Peppe). If you arrive after the TI closes, look for their useful handouts in the lobby of the Foreigners' Club (open until midnight).

To get from the train station to the TI, head straight out to Corso Italia and turn left. Walk five minutes to Piazza Tasso, turn right at the end of the square, and go down Via Luigi de Maio through Piazza Sant'Antonino, bearing right downhill about 30 yards to the Foreigners' Club mansion at #35.

If you just need quick advice, the fake tourist office—located in a green caboose just outside the train station—can be of help. While they're a private business with hopes that you'll purchase one of their overpriced excursions, they're willing to give basic information on directions, buses, and ferries.

Arrival in Sorrento

By Train or Bus: Sorrento is the last stop on the Circumvesuviana train line. In front of the train station is the town's main bus stop, as well as taxis waiting to overcharge you (€15 minimum). All recommended hotels—except those on Via Capo—are within a 10-minute walk.

By Boat: Passenger boats dock at Marina Piccola. To walk from the harbor to Piazza Tasso by the easiest route, follow the *Lift* signs a couple of hundred yards to the elevator. Pay €1 to ride it up into the Villa Comunale city park. From there, exit through the park gate and bear left; Piazza Tasso is about four blocks away. Or, if you don't mind a steep uphill hike, you can hike along the road for 15 minutes (free). Other options are the red-and-white city bus #B or #C (buy €1 tickets at the tobacco shop near the dock, 3/hour); or the small, blue private bus (€1, buy ticket from driver, passes not valid, 4/hour).

By Car: The Achille Lauro underground parking garage is centrally located, just a couple of blocks in front of the train station (€2/hour, €24/24 hours, on Via Correale).

Helpful Hints

Church Services: The **cathedral** hosts an English-language Anglican service at 17:00 most Sundays from June to August. At **Santa Maria delle Grazie** (perhaps the most beautiful Baroque church in town), cloistered nuns sing from above and out of sight during a Mass each morning at 7:30 (on Via delle Grazie).

Bookstore: Libreria Tasso has a decent selection of books in English, including this one (June-Sept daily 10:00-22:00; Oct-May Mon-Sat 9:45-13:00 & 16:00-20:30, Sun 11:00-13:00 & 17:00-20:00; Via San Cesareo 96, one block north of cathedral, near Sorrento Men's Club; tel. 081-807-1639).

Laundry: Sorrento has two handy self-service launderettes (both charge about €8/load wash and dry, includes soap). One launderette is just down the alley next to Corso Italia 30 (daily May-Sept 7:00-24:00, Oct-April 8:00-23:00, Vico I Fuoro 3, mobile 338-506-0942). The other is near the station, at the corner of Corso Italia and Via degli Aranci (daily 7:00-22:00).

Guided Tours of Pompeii, Naples, and Amalfi Coast: Naples-based **Mondo Tours** offers affordable tours of these destinations, including a nine-hour Amalfi Coast drive that starts from Sorrento. You'll sign up in advance and team up with fellow Rick Steves readers to split the cost (making it €45/person).

Local Guides: Giovanna Donadio is a good tour guide for Sorrento, Amalfi, and Capri (€100/half-day, €160/day, same price for any size group, mobile 338-466-0114, giovanna_dona@hotmail.com). **Giovanni Visetti** is a nature lover, mapmaker, and orienteer who organizes hikes and has a fine website describing local trails (mobile 339-694-2911, www.giovis.com, giovis@giovis.com).

Getting Around Sorrento

By Bus: City buses (either orange or red-and-white) all stop near the main square, Piazza Tasso. Bus #A runs east to Meta beach or west to the hotels on Via Capo and beyond; buses #B and #C go to the port (Marina Piccola); and bus #D heads to the fishing village (Marina Grande). Buses #A and #D stop at the beginning of Corso Italia (west side of Piazza Tasso for Via Capo or Marina Grande, east side for Meta); #B and #C stop at the corner of Piazza Sant'Antonino, just down the hill toward the water. The trip between Piazza Tasso and Marina Piccola costs just €1; for other

SORRENTO & CAPRI

Sorrento

Bay of Naples

Marina Grande

Marina San

VILLA COMUNALE PARK & ELEVATOR TO MARINA

Cliffs

SS-145

VIA MARINA GRANDE

To Punta del Capo & Positano

VIA DEL CAPO

B

WALK ENDS

VIA SOPRA LE MURA

VIA DEL MARE

VICO STRETTOLA

V. PAOLO

VIA NASTRO VERDE

VIA CAPODIMONTE

SS-145

SAN NICOLA

SAN VINCENZO

VIA SAN

VIA FUORO

VICO PRIMO FUORO

V. ACC.

VIA TASSO

CORSO ITALIA

OLD WALL

VIA RIVOLO SANT ANTONIO

To Positano

1 Hotel Antiche Mura & Plaza Sorrento

2 Casa Astarita B&B

3 Hotel Mignon

4 Hotel Palazzo Tasso & Kebab Joint

5 Il Palazzo Starace B&B

6 Ulisse Deluxe Hostel

7 Hotel Nice & Penisola Rent

8 Grand Hotel Ambasciatori

9 Hotel Minerva

10 Hotel La Tonnarella & Hotel Désirée

11 Albergo Settimo Cielo

12 Hotel Elios

13 Ristorante il Buco & Teatro Tasso

14 L'Antica Trattoria

15 Inn Bufalito

16 Camera & Cucina Ristorante

SORRENTO & CAPRI

17 Chantecler's Trattoria & Meating	25 Foreigners' Club Rest.
18 Rist. Pizzeria da Gigino	26 Verde Mare
19 Pizzeria da Franco	27 Sorrento Men's Club
20 Decò Supermarket	28 The Fauno Bar
21 Gelateria David	29 The Bagattelle American Bar
22 Gelateria Primavera	30 The English Inn
23 Ristorante Delfino	31 Launderettes (2)
24 Trattoria da Emilia	32 Europcar

trips, tickets cost €2.50 and are good for 45 minutes (purchase at tobacco shops and newsstands). Stamp your ticket upon entering the bus. One-day (€7.60) and three-day bus passes (€18) are also valid on buses along the entire Amalfi Coast.

A different, blue bus (operated by a private company) runs only between the port and Piazza Tasso (4/hour in season, €1, buy ticket from driver); it's not covered by other bus tickets or passes.

By Rental Wheels: Many places rent motor scooters for about €35 per day, including two locations near the train station: **Europcar** (Mon-Sat 9:00-13:00 & 16:00-19:30, Sun by request 10:00-13:00, Corso Italia 210p, tel. 081-878-1386, www.sorrento.it) and **Penisola Rent,** a half-block away (Mon-Sat 9:00-13:00 & 16:00-20:30, Sun 9:00-13:00, located in Hotel Nice, Corso Italia 259, tel. 081-877-4664, www.penisolarent.com). Don't rent a car in summer unless you enjoy traffic jams.

By Taxi: Taxis are expensive, charging an outrageous €15 for the short ride from the station to hotels. Because of heavy traffic and the complex one-way road system, you can often walk faster than you can ride. If you do use a taxi, even if you agree to a set price, be sure it has a meter (all official taxis have one). I think taxis are a huge rip-off, since city officials don't have the nerve to regulate them, and hotels are afraid to alienate them. Walk or take the bus instead.

By Bus Tour: If you'd like to get out of town to see more of the Sorrentine Peninsula, consider **CitySightseeing Sorrento**'s hop-on, hop-off bus tours, with headphone commentary about the two bays flanking this scenic spit of land (€12, 4/day, April-Oct daily, full loop is 1.75 hours, first bus departs from train station at 9:30, buy tickets on board). The pointless **tourist train** you'll see departing from Piazza Tasso loops only through the town itself—all easily reachable by foot (€6, 30-minute tour).

Self-Guided Walk

Welcome to Sorrento

Get to know Sorrento with this lazy self-guided town stroll that ends down by the waterside at the small-boat harbor, Marina Grande.

• *Begin on the main square. Stand under the flags with your back to the sea, and face...*

Piazza Tasso: As in any southern Italian town, this "piazza" is Sorrento's living room. It may be noisy and congested, but locals want to be where the action is...and be part of the scene. The most expensive apartments and top cafés are on or near this square. City buses stop at or close to the square on their way to Marina Piccola and Via Capo. The train station is a five-minute walk to the left. A statue of St. Anthony, patron of Sorrento, faces north as if greeting those coming from Naples (he's often equipped with an armload of fresh lemons and oranges).

This square spans a gorge that divides downtown Sorrento. The newer section (to your left) was farm country just two centuries ago. The older part is to your right, with an ancient Greek gridded street plan (like much of southern Italy, Sorrento was Greek-speaking for centuries before it was Romanized). If you walk a block inland, go right up to the green railing, and look down, you'll see steps that were carved in the fifth century B.C. The combination of the gorge and the seaside cliffs made Sorrento easy to defend. A small section of wall (which you can find near Hotel Mignon) closed the landward gap in the city's defenses.

Sorrento's name may come from the Greek word for "siren," the legendary half-bird, half-woman who sang an intoxicating lullaby. According to Homer, the sirens lived on an island near here. No one had ever sailed by the sirens without succumbing to their incredible musical charms...and to death. But Homer's hero Ulysses was determined to hear the song. He put wax in his oarsmen's ears and had himself lashed to the mast of his ship. Oh, it was nice. The sirens, thinking they had lost their powers, threw themselves into the sea, and the place became safe to inhabit. Ulysses' odyssey was all about the westward expansion of Greek culture, and to the ancient Greeks, places like Sorrento were the wild, wild west.

• *With your back still to the sea, head to the far-right corner of the square, behind the statue of Torquato Tasso, the square's namesake. (A Sorrento native, he was a lively Renaissance poet—but today he seems only to wonder which restaurant to choose for dinner.) Peek into the big courtyard of Palazzo Correale (#18, behind the statue in the right corner) to get a feel for an 18th-century aristocratic palace's courtyard, its walls lined with characteristic tiles. In the same building, you'll see one of the zillions of fun, touristy shops in Sorrento that sells regional goodies and offers free biscuits and tastes of liqueurs. As you're leaving the courtyard, on your immediate left you'll see the narrow...*

Via Santa Maria della Pietà: Here, just a few yards off the noisy main drag, is a street that goes back centuries before Christ. About 100 yards down the lane, at #24 (on the left), find a 13th-century palace (no balconies back then...for security reasons), now an elementary school. A few steps farther on, you'll see a tiny shrine across the street. Typical of southern Italy, it's where the faithful pray to their saint, who contacts Mary, who contacts Jesus, who contacts God. This shrine is a bit more direct—it starts right with Mary.

• *Continue down the lane, which ends at the delightful...*

Cathedral: This is the seat of the local bishop. Pop in for a cool stroll around the ambulatory, checking out the impressive *in-*

tarsio (inlaid-wood) doors. There are two sets of doors—the main entry and the side entry, facing the big street. They're inlaid on both sides and show many scenes of the town and its industry. The doors facing the main street include an old-town map. These were made to celebrate the pope's visit in 1992. Also notice the intricate inlaid Stations of the Cross and the fine *presepe* (manger scene) in the back. This one takes Bethlehem on that first Christmas and sets it in Naples—with pasta, mozzarella, salami, and even Mount Vesuvius in the background (free, daily 8:00-12:30 & 16:30-20:30, no visits during Mass daily at 8:30 and 18:00, plus Sun at 11:00 and 12:15).

• *Backtrack 10 yards down Via Santa Maria della Pietà, turn left, and cross busy Corso Italia. In the summer, this stretch of road is closed to traffic each evening, when it hosts the best of the passeggiata. Look back at the bell tower, with the scavenged ancient Roman columns at its base. Then go straight on Via P. Reginaldo Giuliani (pausing to see who's died lately on the poster board on your right) and follow the...*

Old Greek Street Plan: Locals claim the ancient Greeks laid out the streets east-west for the most sunlight and north-south for the prevailing and cooling breeze.

• *One block ahead, on your right, the 14th-century loggia is home to the...*

Sorrento Men's Club: Once the meeting place of the town's nobles, this club has been a retreat for retired working-class men for generations. Strictly no women— and no phones.

Italian men venerate their mothers. (Italians joke that Jesus must have been a southern Italian because his mother believed her son was God, he believed his mom was a virgin, and he lived at home with her until he was 30.) But Italian men have also built into their culture ways to be on their own. Here, men play cards and gossip under a historic emblem of the city and a finely frescoed 16th-century dome, with its marvelous 3-D scenes.

• *Turn right for a better view of the Men's Club and a historical marker describing the building. Then continue along...*

Via San Cesareo: This touristy pedestrian-only shopping street leads back to Piazza Tasso. It's lined with competitive little shops where you can peruse (and sample) lemon products. Notice the huge ancient doorways with their tiny doors—to let the right people in, carefully, during a more dangerous age.

• *After a block, take a left onto Via degli Archi, go under the arch, and then hang a right (under another arch) to the square with the...*

Statue of St. Anthony (Antonino): Sorrento's town saint humbly looms among the palms, facing the basilica where the reliquary containing a few of his bones lies (free, downstairs in the crypt beneath the altar, surrounded by lots of votives).

• *Exit the square at the bottom-left (following the* lift to the port *signs; don't go down the street with the line of trees and the* porto *signs). After a block or so, on the right you'll see the trees in front of the Imperial Hotel Tramontano, and to their right a path leading to a...*

Cliffside Square: This fine public square, the Villa Comunale, overlooks the harbor. Belly up to the banister to enjoy the view of Marina Piccola and the Bay of Naples. From here, steps zigzag down to the harbor, where lounge chairs, filled by vacationers working on tans, line the sundecks (there's also a €1 elevator to the harbor). The Franciscan church fronting this square faces a fine modern statue of Francis across the street. Next to the church is a dreamy little cloister. Pop inside to see Sicilian Gothic—a 13th-century mix of Norman, Gothic, and Arabic styles, all around the old pepper tree. This is an understandably popular spot for weddings and concerts.

From here, you can quit the walk and stay in the town center, or continue another few minutes downhill to the waterfront at Marina Grande (if it's before 20:00, you'll be able to catch a bus back; otherwise, you'll have to walk back uphill).

• *Return to the road and continue downhill. At the next square (Piazza della Vittoria), which offers another grand view, cut over to the road closest to the water. After winding downhill for a few minutes, it turns into a wide stairway, and just before reaching the waterfront, you pass under an...*

Ancient Greek Gate: This gate marks the boundary between Sorrento and Marina Grande, technically a separate town with its own proud residents—it's said that even their cats look different. Because Marina Grande dwellers lived outside the wall and were more susceptible to rape, pillage, and plunder, Sorrentines believe that they come from Saracen (Turkish pirate) stock. Sorrentines still scare their children by saying, "Behave—or the Turks will take you away."

• *Now go all the way down the steps into Marina Grande, Sorrento's "big" small-boat harbor. (Confusingly, Capri also has a harbor called Marina Grande.)*

Marina Grande: Until recently, this little community was famously traditional, with its economy based on its fishing fleet. Locals recall when women wore black when a relative died (1 year for an uncle, aunt, or sibling; 2-3 years for a husband or parent). Men got off easy, just wearing a black memorial button.

There are two recommended restaurants on the harbor. **Trattoria da Emilia** has an old newspaper clipping, tacked near the

SORRENTO & CAPRI

door, about Sophia Loren filming here. On the far side of the harbor, **Ristorante Delfino** boasts a sundeck for a lazy drink before or after lunch.

• *From here, buses return to the center at Piazza Tasso every hour (€2.50, buy ticket at tobacco shop). Or you can walk back up.*

Sights in Sorrento

▲▲Strolling

Take time to explore the surprisingly pleasant old city between Corso Italia and the sea. Views from Villa Comunale, the public park next to Imperial Hotel Tramontano, are worth the detour. Each night in summer (May-Oct at 19:30; Nov-April weekends only), the police close off Corso Italia to traffic, and Sorrento's main drag becomes a thriving people scene. The *passeggiata* peaks at about 22:00. (When Piazza Tasso

and the main thoroughfare are closed to traffic, buses for Via Capo leave from up on Via degli Aranci, a short walk from Piazza Tasso along Via Fuorimura.)

Lemon Products Galore

Via San Cesareo is lined with hardworking rival shops selling a mind-boggling array of lemon products and offering samples of lots of sour goodies. Poke around for a pungent experience.

▲Lemon Grove Garden (Giardini di Cataldo)

This small park consists of an inviting organic lemon and orange grove lined with shady, welcoming paths. The owners of the grove are seasoned green thumbs, having worked the orchard through many generations. You'll see that they've even grafted orange-tree branches onto a lemon tree so that both fruits now grow on the same tree. The garden is dotted with benches, tables, and an inviting little tasting (and buying) stand. You'll get a chance to sniff and taste the varieties of lemons, and enjoy free samples of chilled *limoncello* along with various other homemade liqueurs made from basil, mandarins, or fennel (enthusiastically free, daily April-Sept 9:30-sunset, Oct-March 10:00-sunset, closed in rainy weather, tel. 081-807-4040, www.igiardinidicataldo.it). The main shop selling their organic homemade products, tasty gelato, and lemonade is across from the Corso Italia entrance at #267; a smaller stand is inside. Enter the garden either on Corso Italia (100 yards north of the train station—where painted tiles show lemon fantasies), or at the intersection of Via Capasso and Via Rota (next to the Hotel La Meridiana Sorrento).

Lemons

Around here, *limoni* are ubiquitous: screaming yellow painted on ceramics, dainty bottles of *limoncello,* and lemons the size of softballs at the fruit stand.

The Amalfi Coast and Sorrento area produces several different kinds of lemons. The gigantic, bumpy "lemons" are actually citrons, called *cedri,* and are more for show—they're pulpier than they are juicy, and make a good marmalade. The juicy *sfusato sorrentino,* grown only in Sorrento, is shaped like an American football, while the *sfusato amalfitano,* with knobby points on both ends, is less juicy but equally aromatic. These two kinds of luscious lemons are used in sweets such as *granita* (shaved ice doused in lemonade), *limoncello* (a candy-like liqueur with a big kick, called *limoncino* on the Cinque Terre), *delizia* (a dome of fluffy cake filled and slathered with a thick whipped lemon cream), *spremuta di limone* (fresh-squeezed lemon juice), and, of course, gelato or *sorbetto alla limone.*

SORRENTO & CAPRI

▲Swimming near Sorrento

If you require immediate tanning, you can rent a chair on a pier by the port. There are no great beaches in Sorrento—the gravelly, jam-packed private beaches of **Marina Piccola** are more for partying than pampering, and there's just a tiny spot for public use. The elevator in Villa Comunale city park (next to the Church of San Francesco) gets you down for €1. At **Marina Grande,** Restaurant Delfino has a pier lined with lounge chairs for sunbathing (free for those with this book who buy lunch there).

There's a classic, sandy Italian beach two miles away at **Meta,** but it's generally overrun by teenagers from Naples. While the Meta Circumvesuviana stop is a very long walk from the beach (or a €25 cab ride), the red-and-white bus #A goes directly from Piazza Tasso to the Meta beach (last stop, schedule posted for hourly returns). At Meta, you'll find pizzerias, snack bars, and a little free section of beach, but the place is mostly dominated by several sprawling private-beach complexes—if you go, pay for a spot in one of these. Lido Metamare seems best (open May-Sept, €2.50 entry; lockable changing cabins, lounge chairs, and more available for an extra fee; tel. 081-532-2505). It's a very Italian scene—locals complain that it's "too local" (i.e., inundated with Naples' riffraff)—with light lunches, a playground, a manicured beach, loud pop music...and no international tourists.

Tarzan might take Jane to the wild and stony beach at **Punta del Capo,** a 15-minute bus ride from Piazza Tasso (the same bus #A explained above, but in the opposite direction from Meta; 2/hour, get off at stop in front of the American Bar, then walk 10 minutes past ruined Roman Villa di Pollio).

Another good choice is **Marina di Puolo,** a tiny fishing town popular in the summer for its sandy beach, surfside restaurants, and beachfront disco (to get here, stay on bus #A a bit farther—ask driver to let you off at Marina di Puolo—then follow signs and hike down about 15 minutes).

Tennis

The Sorrento Sport Snack Bar has two fine courts open to the public (daily 9:30-23:00, until 20:00 in winter, €14/hour including rackets and balls for two people, call for reservation, across from recommended Grand Hotel Ambasciatori at Via Califano 5, tel. 081-807-1616).

Scuba Diving

To escape the shops, dive deep into the Mediterranean. PADI-certified Futuro Mare offers a one-hour boat ride out to the protected marine zone that lies between Sorrento and Capri, where you can try the beginners' dive (€90, includes instruction and complete supervision, April-Oct usually daily at 9:30). The boat also takes experienced certified divers (1 dive-€65, 2 dives-€95, April-Oct daily at 9:30 and 14:00). The whole experience takes about three hours. Prices include all equipment, transportation, and the dive itself, which lasts about 40 minutes for both novices and experts (call a day or two in advance to reserve, tel. 349-653-6323, www.sorrentodiving.it, info@futuromare.it).

Boat Rental

You can rent motor boats big enough for four people (€150/day, plus gas—figure about €30 for a trip to Capri, more with a skipper; with your back to the ferry-ticket offices, it's to the left around the corner at Via Marina Piccola 43; tel. 081-807-2283, www.nauticasicsic.com).

Nightlife in Sorrento

Pubs and Clubs

Sorrento is a fun place to enjoy a drink or some dancing after dinner. The crowd is older, and the many local English expats seem to have paved the way for you.

The Fauno Bar, which dominates Piazza Tasso with tables spilling onto the square, is a fine place to make the scene over a drink any time of day.

The **Bagattelle American Bar,** run by DJ Daniele, who tailors music to the audience, is the oldest club in town. The scene, while sloppy, is generally comfortable with the 30- to 60-year-old crowd. And if you're alone, there's a pole you can dance with (no cover charge, €4-7 drinks, no food, nightly from 21:30, down the steps from the flags at Piazza Tasso).

The **English Inn** offers both a streetside pub and a more re-fined-feeling garden out back—at least until the evening, when the music starts blaring. English vacationers come to Sorrento in droves (many have holidayed here annually for decades). Order up baked beans on toast, €10 fish-and-chips, or just a draft beer (near-ly all drinks-€5, daily, Corso Italia 55, tel. 081-878-2570).

Camera & Cucina, a sleek and modern photography-themed place, offers a snapshot of contemporary Italy with a creative food and drink menu, DJ music late at night, a secluded garden, and people-watching among stylish Italians on vacation (May-Nov daily 18:00-late, Dec-April open Fri-Sat only, reservations smart, Via Correale 19, 4-minute walk from Piazza Tasso, tel. 081-877-3686).

The **Foreigners' Club** offers live Neapolitan songs, Sinatra-style classics, and jazzy elevator music nightly at 20:00 throughout the summer. It's just right for old-timers feeling frisky (in the cen-ter; described earlier under "Helpful Hints").

Theater Show

At **Teatro Tasso,** a hardworking troupe puts on *The Sorrento Musi-cal,* a folk-music show that treats visitors to a schmaltzy dose of Neapolitan Tarantella music and dance—complete with "Funiculì Funiculà" and "Santa Loo-chee-yee-yah." The 75-minute Italian-language extravaganza features a cast of 14 playing guitar, violin, mandolin, and tambourines, and singing operatically from Nea-politan balconies...complete with Vesuvius erupting in the back-ground. Your €25 ticket (or €50 with four-course dinner) includes a drink before and after the show. Maurizio promises my readers a €5 discount if you buy direct from the box office and show this book (maximum 2 tickets per book; mid-April-June and Sept-Oct nightly at 21:30, July-Aug 3-4 nights per week at 21:30, bar opens 30 minutes before show, dinner starts at 20:00 and must be re-served in advance—in person or by email, box office open virtu-ally all day long, theater seats 500, facing Piazza Sant'Antonino in the old town, tel. 081-807-5525, www.teatrotasso.com, info@teatrotasso.com).

Sleeping in Sorrento

Hotels here often charge the same for a room whether it has a view, balcony, or neither. At hotels that offer sea views, ask for a room *"con balcone, con vista sul mare"* (with a balcony, with a sea view). *"Tranquillo"* is taken as a request for a quieter room off the street.

Hotels listed are either near the train station and city center (where balconies overlook city streets) or on cliffside Via Capo (with sea-view balconies). Via Capo is a 20-minute walk—or short bus ride—from the station.

You should have no trouble finding a room any time except in August, when the town is jammed with Italians and prices often rise above the regular high-season rates quoted here. Rates are soft in April and October, and tend to drop by about a third from November to March at the hotels that don't close for the winter. Always contact hotels directly, mention this book, and ask for their best rate. The two holdouts without air-conditioning (Désirée and Elios) are especially good values in April, May, September, and October, when hot temperatures are less likely.

Note: The spindly, more exotic, and more tranquil Amalfi Coast town of Positano (see next chapter) is also a good place to spend the night.

In the Town Center

$$$ Hotel Antiche Mura, with 50 rooms and four stars, is sophisticated, elegant, and plush. It offers all the amenities you could need, including an impressive breakfast buffet. Surrounded by lemon trees, the pool and sundeck are a peaceful oasis. Just a block off the main square, it's quieter than some central hotels because it's perched on the ledge of a dramatic ravine (small-windowed Db-€150, regular Db-€189, balcony Db-€250, Tb-€290, Qb-€340; Michele promises 15 percent off prevailing rates in 2014 if you reserve direct, mention this book, and pay cash; air-con, elevator, Wi-Fi, parking-€10/day, a block inland from Piazza Tasso at Via Fuorimura 7, tel. 081-807-3523, www.hotelantichemura.com, info@hotelantichemura.com).

$$$ Plaza Sorrento is a contemporary-feeling, upscale refuge in the very center of town (next door to Antiche Mura). Its 65 well-soundproofed rooms, arranged on color-coded floors, are mod and minimalist, and the rooftop swimming pool is inviting. Their "comfort" and "superior" rooms offer balconies for €20-40 more (standard Db-€180, elevator, air-con, free Wi-Fi, Via Fuorimura 3, tel. 081-877-1056, www.plazasorrento.com, info@plazasorrento.com).

$$ Casa Astarita B&B is a shining gem in the middle of

Sleep Code

(€1 = about $1.30, country code: 39)
S = Single, **D** = Double/Twin, **T** = Triple, **Q** = Quad, **b** = bathroom, **s** = shower only. Unless otherwise noted, credit cards are accepted, English is spoken, and breakfast is included. A local tax of €1 per person, per night (more for fancier hotels) is not included in these rates.

To help you sort easily through these listings, I've divided the accommodations into three categories based on the price for a standard double room with bath:

$$$ Higher Priced—Most rooms €140 or more.
  $$ Moderately Priced—Most rooms between €85-140.
    $ Lower Priced—Most rooms €85 or less.

Prices can change without notice; verify the hotel's current rates online or by email. For the best prices, always book direct.

town, with a crazy-quilt-tiled entryway. You'll find six bright, tranquil, air-conditioned rooms (three with little balconies) and a fully stocked communal fridge and sideboard for help-yourself breakfasts in the rustic-yet-elegant common room. Despite double-paned windows, pub noise can seep into the three front-facing, balcony rooms (Db-€115, Tb-€130, air-con, guest computer, free Wi-Fi, 50 yards past the cathedral on Corso Italia at #67, tel. 081-877-4906, www.casastarita.com, info@casastarita.com, Annamaria and Alfonso). If there's no one at reception, ask at Hotel Mignon (described next)—the same family runs both hotels.

$$ Hotel Mignon rents 24 soothing blue rooms with pretty, tiled public spaces in a quiet, central location near the cathedral (Sb-€80, Db-€105, big Db-€120, Tb-€130, these prices good with this book when you reserve direct, air-con, guest computer, free Wi-Fi, rooftop sundeck, some balconies but no views; from the cathedral, walk a block farther up Corso Italia and look for the hotel up a small gated lane to your left; Via Sersale 9, tel. 081-807-3824, www.sorrentohotelmignon.com, info@sorrentohotelmignon.com, Paolo).

$$ Hotel Palazzo Tasso is a simple, new place with a good location and 11 sleek, modern, reasonably priced rooms, though there's very little public space (Db-€90, up to €140 in peak season, air-con, small breakfast room on top floor, open all year, Via Santa Maria della Pietà 33, tel. 081-878-3579, www.palazzotasso.com, info@palazzotasso.com).

$$ Il Palazzo Starace B&B offers seven tidy rooms in a little alley off Corso Italia (opposite Hotel del Corso, listed earlier), one block from Piazza Tasso (Db-€90, nicer balcony Db-€110, five-bed family room-€150, 10 percent off with cash and this book in 2014, air-con, no elevator but a luggage dumbwaiter, free Wi-Fi; ring bell around corner from Via Santa Maria della Pietà 9, then climb 3 floors; tel. 081-807-2633, mobile 366-950-5377, www.palazzostarace.com, info@palazzostarace.com, Massimo).

$ Ulisse Deluxe Hostel is the best budget deal in town. This "hostel" is actually a hotel, with 56 marble-tiled rooms and elegant public areas, but also has two eight-bed dorm rooms (hotel: Db-€80, Tb-€120, Qb-€150; hostel: €25/bunk in single-sex dorm; both types of rooms include morning coffee, breakfast buffet-€7, these rates valid when you mention this book and reserve direct, air-con, elevator, free Wi-Fi, spa and pool use extra, parking-€10/day, Via del Mare 22, tel. 081-877-4753, www.ulissedeluxe.com, info@ulissedeluxe.com, Chiara). The hostel is a 5-minute walk from the old-town action, hiding beneath a big parking lot—go downhill along the right side of the lot to find the entrance.

$ Hotel Nice rents 29 simple, cramped, cheap rooms with high ceilings 100 yards in front of the train station on the noisy main drag. This last resort is worth considering only for its very handy-to-the-train-station location. Alfonso promises that you can have a quiet room—which is critical given the thin windows and busy location—if you request it with your booking email (Sb-€50, €60 in Aug; Db-€75, €85 in Aug; extra bed-€20; 10 percent discount when you book direct, mention this book, and pay cash; air-con, elevator, rooftop terrace, free Wi-Fi, closed Nov-March, Corso Italia 257, tel. 081-878-1650, www.hotelnice.it, info@hotelnice.it).

At the East End of Town

This hotel is only a few minutes' walk beyond the town center. To reach it, head a block in front of the train station, turn right onto Corso Italia, then left down Via Capasso (which eventually winds right and becomes Via Califano).

$$$ Grand Hotel Ambasciatori is a sumptuous four-star hotel with 100 rooms, a cliffside setting, a sprawling garden, and a pool. This is Humphrey Bogart land, with plush public spaces, a relaxing stay-awhile ambience, and a free elevator to its "private beach"—actually a sundeck built out over the water (prices vary wildly, but in high season generally: viewless Db-€200, sea-view Db-€350, 10 percent discount with this book if you book direct, also check website for specials, elevator, air-con in summer, balconies in most rooms, pay guest computer, free Wi-Fi, parking-€20/day, closed Nov-March, Via Califano 18, tel. 081-878-2025, www.ambasciatorisorrento.com, ambasciatori@manniellohotels.com).

With a View on Via Capo

These cliffside hotels are outside of town, toward the cape of the peninsula (from the train station, go straight out Corso Italia, which turns into Via Capo). Once you're set up, commuting into town by bus or on foot is easy. Hotel Minerva is my favorite Sorrento splurge, while Hotel Désirée and Hotel Elios are super budget bets and have comparable views. If you're in Sorrento to stay put and luxuriate, especially with a car, these accommodations are perfect (although I'd rather luxuriate in Positano—see next chapter).

Getting to Via Capo: From the city center, it's a gradually uphill 15-minute walk (20 minutes from train station, last part is a bit steeper), a €20 taxi ride, or a cheap bus ride. If you're arriving with luggage, you can wait at the train station for one of the long-distance SITA buses (usually blue or green-and-white) that stop on Via Capo on their way to Massa Lubrense (about every 40 minutes; don't take the ones heading for Positano/Amalfi). Frequent Sorrento city buses leave from Piazza Tasso in the city center, a five-minute walk from the station (go down a block and turn left on Corso Italia; from far side of the piazza, look for red-and-white bus #A, about 3/hour). Tickets for either bus are sold at the station newsstand and tobacco shops (€2.50). Get off at the Hotel Belair stop for the hotels listed here. If you're headed to Via Capo after 19:30, when the center (and Piazza Tasso bus stop) is closed to traffic, catch the bus instead on Via degli Aranci (with your back to the station, wind left, up and around it; the bus stop is near Bar Paradise).

Getting from Via Capo into Town: Buses work great once you get the hang of them (and it's particularly gratifying to avoid the taxi racket). To reach downtown Sorrento from Via Capo, catch any bus heading downhill from Hotel Belair (3/hour, buses run all day and evening).

$$$ Hotel Minerva is like a sun-worshipper's temple. The road-level entrance (on a busy street) leads to an elevator that takes you to the fifth-floor reception. Getting off, you'll step onto a spectacular terrace with outrageous Mediterranean views. Bright common areas, a small rooftop swimming pool, and a cold-water Jacuzzi complement 60 large, tiled, colorful rooms with views, some with balconies (Db-€160, Tb-€200, these discounted prices promised through 2014 if you reserve direct and mention this book, can be cheaper in shoulder season, air-con, guest computer, free Wi-Fi, parking-€15/day, closed Nov-March, Via Capo 30, tel. 081-878-1011, www.minervasorrento.com, minerva@acampora.it).

$$$ Hotel La Tonnarella is an old-time Sorrentine villa turned boutique hotel, with several terraces, stylish tiles, and indifferent service. Eighteen of its 24 rooms have views of the sea (non-view Db-€140, "superior" sea-view or balcony Db-€180, "deluxe"

Db with view terrace-€205, exotic view suite with terrace-€320, email or check website for best rates, extra bed-€30, €30/person half-pension available, air-con, guest computer, free Wi-Fi, no elevator in building, parking-€5/day, small beach with private elevator access, closed Nov-March, Via Capo 31, tel. 081-878-1153, www.latonnarella.it, info@latonnarella.it).

$$ Albergo Settimo Cielo ("Seventh Heaven") is an old-fashioned, family-run cliff-hanger sitting 300 steps above Marina Grande. The reception is just off the waterfront side of the road, and the elevator passes down through four floors with 50 clean but spartan rooms—all with grand views, and many with balconies. The rooms feel dated for the price—you're paying for the views (Sb-€120, Db-€140, Tb-€180, Qb-€215, check website for specials, mention this book for 5 percent discount on these rates when reserving direct, air-con in summer, guest computer, free Wi-Fi, free parking with this book, inviting pool in the summer, sun terrace, closed Nov-March, Via Capo 27, tel. 081-878-1012, www.hotelsettimocielo.com, info@hotelsettimocielo.com; Giuseppe, sons Stefano and Massimo, and daughter Serena).

$$ Hotel Désirée is a modest affair, with reasonable rates, humbler vistas, and no traffic noise. The 22 basic rooms have high, ravine-facing or partial-sea views, and half come with balconies (all the same price). Most rooms have fans, and there's a fine rooftop sunning terrace and lovable cats. Owner Corinna (a committed environmentalist), daughter Cassandra, and receptionist Antonio serve an all-organic breakfast and are hugely helpful with tips on exploring the peninsula (Sb-€62, small Db-€77, Db-€87, Tb-€107, Qb-€117, lots of stairs with no elevator, guest computer, free Wi-Fi, laundry-€8, free parking, shares driveway and beach elevator with La Tonnarella, closed early Nov-mid-Dec and early Jan-Feb yet open for Christmas—rare for this area, Via Capo 31, tel. 081-878-1563, www.desireehotelsorrento.com, info@desireehotelsorrento.com).

$ Hotel Elios, warmly run by Gianna, is humble...much like a Sorrentine *nonna*'s house. It offers 14 simple but spacious rooms—12 with balconies and views—a panoramic sun terrace, and a quiet atmosphere. She serves a small continental breakfast, and you're welcome to use the kitchen and dining room (Sb-€55, Db-€85, Tb-€105, extra bed-€25, family rooms, cash only, free Wi-Fi in common areas, free parking, closed mid-Nov-mid-March, Via Capo 33, tel. 081-878-1812, www.hotelelios.it, info@hotelelios.it).

Eating in Sorrento

Gourmet Splurges Downtown

In a town proud to have no McDonald's, consider eating well for a few extra bucks. Both of these places are worthwhile splurges run by a hands-on boss with a passion for good food and exacting service. The first is gourmet and playful. The second is classic. Both are romantic. Be prepared to relax and stay a while.

Ristorante il Buco, once the cellar of an old monastery, is now a small, dressy restaurant that serves delightfully presented, playful, and creative modern Mediterranean dishes under a grand, rustic arch. Peppe and his staff love to explain exactly what's on the plate. The dashing team of cooks builds sophisticated dishes with an emphasis on seafood in a state-of-the-art kitchen. Peppe, who holds the only Michelin star in town, designs his menu around whatever's fresh. Reservations are often necessary to sit inside under their elegant vault (€18-24 pastas, €25-28 *secondi*, dinners run from about €50 plus wine, extravagant tasting *menu*s for €60-100, 10 percent discount when you show this book, always a good vegetarian selection, Thu-Tue 12:30-14:30 & 19:30-22:30, closed Wed and Jan; just off Piazza Sant'Antonino—facing the basilica, go under the grand arch on the left and immediately enter the restaurant at II Rampa Marina Piccola 5; tel. 081-878-2354, www.ilbucoristorante.it).

L'Antica Trattoria serves more traditional cuisine from an inviting but pricey menu in a *romantico* candlelit ambience. The atmosphere is sedate and a bit old-school pretentious, with formally attired waiters. Run by the same family since 1930, the restaurant has a trellised garden outside and intimate nooks inside (perhaps too isolated for some, but ideal for small groups). Walk around the labyrinthine interior before you select a place to sit. Aldo and sons will take care of you while Vincenzo, the Joe Cocker-esque resident mandolin player, entertains. They offer several fixed-price meals (including a €20 two-course lunch and a €35 four-course dinner, 10 percent discount on these meals when you show this book), or you can order à la carte (€15-20 pastas, €26-29 *secondi*). Show this book for a free *limoncello* to cap the experience (always good vegetarian options, daily 12:00-23:30, closed Mon Nov-Feb, air-con, reservations smart, Via Padre R. Giuliani 33, tel. 081-807-1082).

Mid-Priced Restaurants Downtown

Inn Bufalito specializes in *mozzarella di bufala*, of course, but also features all things buffalo—steak, sausage, salami, carpaccio, buffalo-meat pasta sauce, and several different types of buffalo milk cheese. They serve more standard Italian food, too, but the buffalo theme is the reason to come. The smartly designed space has a modern, borderline-trendy, casual atmosphere and a fun indoor-outdoor vibe (€6-9 salads, €8-10 pastas, €9-14 *secondi,* no cover, don't miss the seasonal specialties on the blackboard, daily 12:00-24:00, closed Oct-April, Vico I Fuoro 21, tel. 081-365-6975).

Camera & Cucina is less traditional and more expensive, with mod atmosphere, a fine garden, and a creative menu that caters to trendy young locals (€9-13 pastas, €15-18 *secondi,* May-Nov daily 18:00-late, Dec-April open Fri-Sat only, reservations smart, Via Correale 19, 4-minute walk from Piazza Tasso, tel. 081-877-3686).

Chantecler's Trattoria, a hole-in-the-wall, family-run place on the narrow lane that leads to the cathedral, is particularly great for meat and vegetarian fare. They offer a €9 meal deal at lunch: your choice of one *primo* and one *secondo* (prices slightly higher at dinner—€7 pastas, €10 *secondi,* no cover charge, good vegetarian dishes, take out or eat in, Tue-Sun 12:00-15:00 & 19:00-24:00, closed Mon, Via Santa Maria della Pietà 38, tel. 081-807-5868, Luigi and family).

Ristorante Pizzeria da Gigino, lively and congested with a sprawling interior and tables spilling onto the street, makes huge, tasty Neapolitan-style pizzas in their wood-burning oven (€8-10 pizzas and pastas, €8-13 *secondi,* no cover charge, daily 12:00-24:00, closed Jan-Feb; just off Piazza Sant'Antonino—take first road to the left of Sant'Antonino as you face him, pass under the archway, and take the first left to Via degli Archi 15; tel. 081-878-1927, Antonino).

Meating, as its name implies, focuses on top-quality meats, from homemade sausages to giant steaks on a wood-fired grill. You'll find no seafood or pasta here, but there are a variety of vegetable dishes and delicious local cheeses, along with a reasonably priced selection of wine (€10-18 steaks, daily 18:00-24:00, Via Santa Maria della Pietà 20, tel. 081-878-2891).

With a Sea View: The **Foreigners' Club Restaurant** has some of the best sea views in town (with a sprawling terrace under breezy palms), live music nightly at 20:00 (May-mid-Oct), and passable meals. It's a good spot for dessert or an after-dinner *limoncello* (€9-14 pastas and pizzas, €12-23 *secondi,* daily, bar opens at 9:30, meals served 11:00-23:00, Via Luigi de Maio 35, tel. 081-877-3263). If you'd enjoy eating along the water (rather than just with a water view), see "Harborside in Marina Grande," later.

Cheap Eats Downtown

Pizza: **Pizzeria da Franco** seems to be Sorrento's favorite place for basic, casual pizza in a fun, untouristy atmosphere. There's nothing fancy about this place—just locals on benches eating hot sandwiches and great pizzas served on waxed paper in a square tin. It's packed to the rafters with a youthful crowd that doesn't mind the plastic cups (€6-8 pizzas and calzones, €5-7 salads, takeout possible, daily 8:00-2:00 in the morning, just across from Lemon Grove Garden on busy Corso Italia at #265, tel. 081-877-2066).

Kebabs: **Kebab Joint,** a little hole-in-the-wall, has a passionate following among eaters who appreciate Andrea's fresh bread, homemade sauces, and ethic of buying meat fresh each day (and closing when the supply is gone). This is your best non-Italian €5 meal in town. Choose beef or chicken—locals don't go for pork—and garnish as you like with fries and/or salad (nightly from 17:00, before the cathedral off Via Santa Maria della Pietà, at Vico il Traversa Pietà 23, tel. 081-807-4595).

Picnics: Get groceries at the **Decò supermarket** (Mon-Sat 8:30-20:30, Sun 9:30-13:00 & 16:30-20:00, Corso Italia 223).

Gelato: Near the train station, **Gelateria David** has many repeat customers (so many flavors, so little time). In 1957, Augusto Davide opened a *gelateria* in Sorrento, and his grandson, Mario, proudly carries on the tradition today (the gelato is still made onsite). Before choosing, sample *Profumi di Sorrento* (an explosive sorbet of mixed fruits), "Sorrento moon" (white almond with lemon zest), and lemon crème. They also serve sandwiches at fair prices (€2 cones, daily 9:00-24:00, shorter hours in spring and fall, closed Dec-Feb, a block below the train station at Via Marziale 19, tel. 081-807-3649). Mario also offers gelato-making classes for a behind-the-scenes look at Italy's favorite dessert (€10/person, 5-person minimum, 1 hour, call or email ahead to reserve, gelateria-david@yahoo.it). Don't mistake this place for the similarly named Gelateria Davide, in the town center—owned by a distant relative, but not as good.

At **Gelateria Primavera,** another local favorite, Antonio and Alberta whip up 70 exotic flavors—and still have time to make pastries for the pope (and everybody else—check out the photos). Try the *noci* (pronounced NO-chee) *di Sorrento,* made from local walnuts (€2.50 cones, daily 9:00-24:00, just west of Piazza Tasso at Corso Italia 142, tel. 081-807-3252).

Harborside in Marina Grande

For a decent dinner *con vista,* head down to either of these restaurants by Sorrento's small-boat harbor, Marina Grande. To get to Marina Grande, follow the directions from the cliffside square on the "Welcome to Sorrento" walk (described earlier). For a less scenic route, walk down Via del Mare, past the recommended Ulisse Deluxe Hostel, to the harbor. Either way, it's about a 15-minute stroll from downtown. You can also take bus #D from Piazza Tasso (€2.50).

Ristorante Delfino serves fish in big portions to hungry locals in a quiet and bright, Seattle-style pier restaurant. The cooking, service, and setting are all top-notch. The restaurant is lovingly run by Luisa, her brothers Andrea and Roberto, and her husband Antonio. Show this book for a free glass of *limoncello* to cap the meal. If you're here for lunch, take advantage of the sundeck—show this book to get an hour of relaxation and digestion on the lounge chairs (€11-16 pastas, €17-30 *secondi*, daily 11:30-15:30 & 18:30-23:00, closed Nov-March; at Marina Grande, facing the water, go all the way to the left and follow signs; tel. 081-878-2038).

Trattoria da Emilia, at the opposite end of the tranquil Marina Grande waterfront, is considerably more rustic, less expensive, and good for straightforward, typical Sorrentine home-cooking, including fresh fish, lots of fried seafood, and *gnocchi di mamma*—potato dumplings with meat sauce, basil, and mozzarella (€7-12 pastas, €11-15 *secondi*, daily 12:15-15:00 & 19:00-22:30, Sept-Oct closed Tue, closed Nov-Feb, no reservations taken, indoor and outdoor seating, tel. 081-807-2720).

On Via Capo
Verde Mare is the locals' pick for a reasonably priced meal (Thu-Tue 12:30-14:45 & 19:00-23:30, closed Wed, 300 yards uphill from La Tonnarella and other recommended hotels, tel. 081-878-2589).

Sorrento Connections

It's impressively fast to zip by boat from Sorrento to most coastal towns and islands during the summer, when there are many more departures. In fact, it's quicker and easier for residents to get around by fast boat than by car or train.

By Train and Bus
From Sorrento to Naples, Pompeii, and Herculaneum by Circumvesuviana Train: This commuter train runs twice hourly between Naples and Sorrento (www.vesuviana.it). From Sorrento, it's about 30 minutes to Pompeii, 50 minutes to Herculaneum (€2.20 one-way for either trip), and 70 minutes to Naples (€4.20 one-way). There's no round-trip discount, and the €12 all-day pass is generally not worthwhile (except on weekends, when it's called a "weekend pass" and is roughly half-price—€6.50). If there's a line at the train station, you can also buy tickets at the appropriately named Snack Bar (across from the main ticket office) or downstairs at the newsstand.

When returning to Naples' Centrale Station on the Circumvesuviana, get off at the next-to-the-last station, Garibaldi (Centrale Station is just up the escalator). Bonus: When returning from Sorrento, your Circumvesuviana ticket includes travel on the Naples Metro or bus system within three hours of validation (no need to validate again). The trip is also covered by the Campania ArteCard. The schedule is printed in the free *Surrentum* magazine (available at TI). Note that the risk of theft is mostly limited to suburban Naples, but can be a problem anywhere. Going between Sorrento and Pompeii or Herculaneum is generally safer.

From Sorrento to Naples Airport: Six Curreri buses run daily to and from the airport; confirm the schedule at the TI (€10, pay driver, daily at 6:30, 8:30, 10:30, 12:00, 14:00, and 16:30, likely 2 additional departures May-Oct, 1.5 hours, departs from in front of train station, tel. 081-801-5420, www.curreriviaggi.it). Although it's possible to connect through Naples (either take a jet boat/hydrofoil to Naples, then cross the street to catch the airport bus on Piazza Municipio; or ride the Circumvesuviana to Naples' Centrale Station to catch the airport bus from Piazza Garibaldi), the direct bus is more convenient and reliable.

From Sorrento to Rome: Most people ride the Circumvesuviana 70 minutes to Naples, then catch the Frecciarossa express train to Rome. However, the Sorrento-Rome bus is direct, cheaper, and all on one ticket—although the departure times can be inconvenient. Buses leave Sorrento's train station and arrive at Rome's Tiburtina station (€18, Mon-Sat at 6:00 and 17:00, Sun at 17:00, off-season at 6:00 only, 4 hours; buy tickets at www.marozzivt.it—in Italian only, at some travel agencies, or on board for a €3 surcharge; tel. 080-579-0111). A Curreri bus makes the trip as well, but only in the summer (departs Mon-Sat at 6:30, 4 hours, tel. 081-801-5420, www.curreriviaggi.it).

By Boat

The number of boats that run per day varies according to the season. The frequency indicated here is for roughly mid-May through mid-October, with more boats per day in the peak of summer and fewer off-season. Check all schedules with the TI, your hotel, or online (use the individual boat company websites—see below—or visit www.capritourism.com, select English, and click on "Shipping timetable"). The Caremar line, a subsidized state-run ferry company, takes cars, offers fewer departures, and is just a bit slower—but cheaper—than the hydrofoil. All of the boats take several hundred people each—and frequently fill up. Boat tickets are sold only at the port.

From Sorrento to Capri: Boats run at least hourly. Your options include a fast **ferry** (*traghetto* or *nave veloce,* 4/day, 25 minutes, €15, run by Caremar, tel. 081-807-3077, www.caremar.it) or a slightly faster, pricier **hydrofoil** (*aliscafi,* up to 20/day, 20 minutes, €17-18, run by Gescab, tel. 081-807-1812, www.gescab.it). To minimize the crowds on Capri, it's best to buy your ticket at 8:00 and take the 8:25 hydrofoil (if you miss it, try to depart by 9:30 at the very latest). These early boats can be jammed, but it's worth it once you reach the island.

From Sorrento to Other Points: Naples (6/day, departs roughly every 2 hours, 35 minutes, €12-13, starting at 7:20), **Positano** (mid-April-mid-Oct only, 2-4/day, 35 minutes, €16), **Amalfi** (mid-April-mid-Oct only, 2-4/day, 1.25 hours, €21).

Getting to Sorrento's Port: To walk from Sorrento's Piazza Tasso to Marina Piccola (the port), you have three options: Go down the stairs near the statue's left side (about 10 minutes); take the slightly longer road (with fewer stairs) that passes by the TI and Foreigners' Club; or find the Villa Comunale public park (see the self-guided tour, earlier) and take the stairs or elevator (€1) down from there. You also can take a bus: From Piazza Sant'Antonino, catch a red-and-white bus #B or #C (3/hour, €1, buy ticket at tobacco shop and specify that you're going to the *porto*) or the little blue bus (4/hour, €1, buy ticket from driver).

Capri

Capri was made famous as the vacation hideaway of Roman emperors Augustus and Tiberius. In the 19th century, it was the haunt of Romantic Age aristocrats on their Grand Tour of Europe. Later it was briefly a refuge for Europe's artsy gay community: Oscar Wilde, D. H. Lawrence, and company hung out here back when being gay could land you in jail...or worse. And these days, the island is a world-class tourist trap, packed with gawky, nametag-wearing visitors searching for the rich and famous—and finding only their prices.

The "Island of Dreams" is a zoo in July and August—overrun with tacky, low-grade group tourism at its worst. At other times of the year, though still crowded, it can provide a relaxing and scenic break from the cultural gauntlet of Italy.

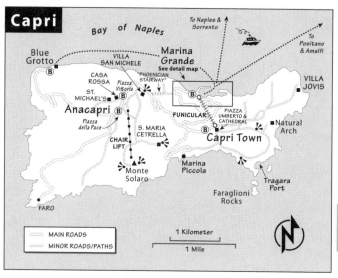

Planning Your Time

This is the best see-everything-in-a-day plan from Naples or Sorrento: Take an early hydrofoil to Capri (from Sorrento, buy ticket at 8:00, boat leaves at 8:25 and arrives at 8:45—smart). Go directly by boat to the Blue Grotto. Instead of taking the boat back, catch a bus from the grotto to Anacapri, which has two or three hours' worth of sightseeing. In Anacapri, see the town, ride the chairlift to Monte Solaro and back (or hike down), stroll out from the base of the chairlift to Villa San Michele for the view, and eat lunch. Afterward, catch a bus to Capri town, which is worth at least a half-hour. Finally, ride the funicular from Capri town down to the harbor and laze on the free beach or wander the yacht harbor while waiting for your boat.

If you're heading to Capri specifically to see the Blue Grotto, be sure to check the weather and sea conditions. If the tide is too high or the water too rough, the grotto can be closed. Ask the TI or your hotelier before going.

Efficient travelers can see Capri on the way between destinations: Sail from Sorrento, check your bag at the harbor, see Capri, and take a boat directly from there to Naples (or vice versa).

If you buy a one-way ticket to Capri (there's no round-trip discount anyway), you'll have maximum schedule flexibility and can take any convenient hydrofoil or ferry back. (Check times for the last return crossing upon arrival with any TI on Capri, or at www.capritourism.com; the last return trips usually leave between 18:30 and 19:30.) During July and August, however, it's wise to get a round-trip boat ticket with a late return time (ensuring you a spot on a boat at the time they're most crowded)—you can always use the ticket to return earlier if you like. Be 20 minutes early for the boat, or you can be bumped.

Starting your day as early as reasonably possible is key to an enjoyable trip to Capri. Day-trippers come down from as far as Rome, creating a daily rush hour in each direction (arriving between 10:00-11:00, leaving around 17:00). If you arrive before them, the entire trip to and into the Blue Grotto might take just a half-hour; arrive later and you might face as much as a two-hour delay.

Orientation to Capri

First thing—pronounce it right: Italians say KAH-pree, not kah-PREE like the song or the pants. The island is small—just four miles by two miles—and is separated from the Sorrentine Peninsula by a narrow strait. Home to 13,000 people, there are only two towns to speak of: Capri and Anacapri. The island also has some scant Roman ruins and a few interesting churches and villas. But its chief attraction is its famous Blue Grotto, and its best activity is the chairlift from Anacapri up the island's Monte Solaro.

Tourist Information

Capri's efficient English-speaking tourist information office has branches in Marina Grande, Capri town, and Anacapri. Their well-organized website has schedules and practical information in English (www.capritourism.com).

The **Marina Grande TI** is by the Motoscafisti Capri tour boat dock (May-Sept Mon-Sat 9:30-13:30 & 15:30-18:45, Sun 9:00-15:00; Oct-April generally daily 9:00-15:00; pick up free map—or the better €1 map if you'll be venturing to the outskirts of Capri town or Anacapri, tel. 081-837-0634).

The **Capri town TI** fills a closet under the bell tower on Piazza Umberto and is less crowded than its sister at the port (Mon-Sat 9:30-13:30 & 15:30-18:45, Sun 9:00-15:00, shorter hours off-season, WC and baggage storage downstairs behind TI, tel. 081-837-0686).

The tiny **Anacapri TI** is at Via Orlandi 59 (Mon-Sat 9:00-15:00, closed Sun, may be closed Nov-Easter, tel. 081-837-1524).

Arrival in Capri

Approaching Capri: Get oriented on the boat before you dock, as you near the harbor with the island spread out before you. The port is a small community of its own, called **Marina Grande,** connected by a funicular and buses to the rest of the island. **Capri**

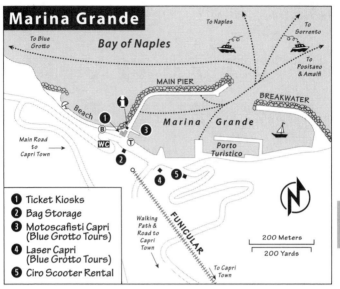

Marina Grande

Bay of Naples

To Naples

To Sorrento

To Blue Grotto

To Positano & Amalfi

MAIN PIER

BREAKWATER

Beach

Marina   Grande

Main Road to Capri Town

WC

Porto Turistico

❶ Ticket Kiosks
❷ Bag Storage
❸ Motoscafisti Capri (Blue Grotto Tours)
❹ Laser Capri (Blue Grotto Tours)
❺ Ciro Scooter Rental

Walking Path & Road to Capri Town

FUNICULAR

To Capri Town

200 Meters

200 Yards

SORRENTO & CAPRI

town fills the ridge high above the harbor. The ruins of Emperor Tiberius' palace, **Villa Jovis,** cap the peak on the left. To the right, the dramatic *"Mamma mia!"* road arcs around the highest mountain on the island **(Monte Solaro),** leading up to **Anacapri** (the island's second town, just out of sight). Notice the old zigzag steps below that road. Until 1874, this was the only connection between Capri and Anacapri. (Though it's quite old, it's nowhere near as old as its nickname, "The Phoenician Stairway," implies.) The white house on the ridge above the zigzags is **Villa San Michele** (where you can go later for a grand view of boats like the one you're on now).

Arrival at Marina Grande: Upon arrival, get your bearings. Find the base of the **funicular railway** (signed *funicolare*) that runs up to Capri town, and stand facing it, with your back to the water.

The fourth little clothing-and-souvenir shop to the right of the funicular provides **baggage storage** (look inside for *left luggage* sign on far back wall, €3/bag, daily 9:00-18:00, tel. 081-837-4575). If it's closed, your best option is at the upper funicular station in Capri town (bag storage near public WCs, €3/bag, daily 7:00-20:00; be aware that you may have to pay extra to take big bags up the funicular).

To your right is a stand of ticket windows with counters for **funicular and bus tickets** (you can't buy tickets at the funicular itself) and for return **boat tickets** to Naples and Sorrento. Just beyond these is the **stop for buses** to the rest of the island. Across the street is a **public WC** (€0.50), and a little farther on is Marina Grande's pebbly public beach.

Two competing companies offer **boat trips** around the island and to the Blue Grotto: Laser Capri and Motoscafisti Capri. You'll see Motoscafisti Capri's dock and ticket shed near the ticket windows; Laser Capri's office is halfway down the waterfront to the left at Via Cristoforo Colombo 69. Both offer similar services (see "Getting Around Capri," later).

The **TI** is near the ticket kiosks, right by the Motoscafisti Capri dock (for TI details, see "Tourist Information," earlier).

From the port, you can take a boat to the Blue Grotto (my recommended plan) or around the island, the funicular to Capri town, or a bus to various destinations on Capri. If you have energy to burn, you can follow the steep paved footpath that connects the port area with Capri town. It starts a block inland from the ferry dock (follow the signs to *Capri centro*; allow 30 minutes).

Helpful Hints

Cheap Tricks: A cheap day trip to Capri is tough. Hydrofoils from Sorrento or Naples cost €15 to €20 each way, and Blue Grotto tickets (plus boat transportation) come to €26—that's €56-66 per person. Taking the slightly slower Caremar ferry to Capri instead of the hydrofoil saves about €3-5 per person each way, and using the bus to the Blue Grotto saves about €6 (see "Blue Grotto," later). After the boats stop running, anyone willing to swim the few yards in from the little dock can see the Blue Grotto for free (albeit illegally).

Best Real Hike: Serious hikers love the peaceful and scenic three-hour Fortress Hike, which takes you entirely away from the tourists. You'll walk under ruined forts along the rugged coast, from the Blue Grotto to the *faro* (lighthouse). From there, you can take a bus back to Anacapri (3/hour). The tourist office has a fine map/brochure.

Free Beach: Marina Grande has a free pebbly beach. You can get a shower at the bar for €1.

Local Guides: Anna Bilardi Leva lives on Capri and is licensed to guide both on the island, and elsewhere around Naples (€130/half-day, €200/day, mobile 339-712-7416, www.capritourinformation.com, annaleva@hotmail.it). **Giovanna Donadio** is a good tour guide for Sorrento, Amalfi, and Capri (€100/half-day, €160/day, same price for any size group, mobile 338-466-0114, giovanna_dona@hotmail.com). Naples-based **Pina Esposito** also does tours of the entire region.

Getting Around Capri

By Bus and Funicular: Tickets for the island's buses and funicular cost €1.80 per ride or €8.60 for an all-day pass (includes deposit—turn it in at the end of the day to get €1 back). Single-ride tickets are available at newsstands, tobacco shops, official ticket offices, or from the driver. All-day passes and funicular tickets are usually sold only at official ticket offices. The all-day pass pays for itself if you take at least five rides on the buses and funicular (possible if you go by bus to the Blue Grotto and spend some time in both towns).

Schedules are clearly posted at all bus stations. Buses from the port to Capri town, and from Capri town to Anacapri, are frequent (4/hour, 10 minutes). The direct bus between the port to Anacapri runs less often (every 30-40 minutes, 25 minutes). From Anacapri, branch bus lines run to the parking lot above the Blue Grotto and to the Faro lighthouse. Buses are teeny (because of the island's narrow roads) and often packed. At most stops, you'll see ranks for passengers to line up in. Drivers can push a button to change the bus's display to *completo* (full), in which case you just have to wait for the next one.

By Taxi: Taxis have fixed rates (Marina Grande to Capri town-€15; Marina Grande to Anacapri-€20 for 3 people, €2/additional person). You can hire a taxi for about €70 per hour—negotiate.

Scooter Rental: If you are experienced at riding a scooter, this is the perfect way to have the run of the island. (For novice riders, Capri's steep and narrow roads aren't a good place to start.) **Ciro** proudly rents bright-yellow scooters with 50cc engines—strong enough to haul couples. Rental includes a map and instructions with parking tips and other helpful information (€15/hour, €55/day, €5 discount with this book for 2 hours or more in 2014; includes helmet, gas, and insurance; daily April-Oct 9:30-19:00, may open in good weather off-season, look for the Ferrari logo at Via Don Giobbe Ruocco 55, Marina Grande, tel. 081-837-8018, mobile 338-360-6918, www.capriscooter.com).

Boat Trips Around the Island: Both **Laser Capri** and **Motoscafisti Capri** run quick one-hour trips that circle the island, passing stunning cliffs, caves, and views that most miss when they go only to the Blue Grotto (€16-17; see contact details under "Blue Grotto," later). With both companies, you can combine the boat trip with a visit to the Blue Grotto at no extra charge (figure another hour). As the trip just to the grotto already costs €13.50, the island circle is well worth the extra €3 if you have an hour to spare (boats leave daily from 9:00 until 13:00 or possibly later—whenever Blue Grotto rowboats stop running).

Sights in Capri

Capri Town

This is a cute but extremely clogged and touristy shopping town. It's worth a brief visit, including the Giardini Augusto, before moving on to more interesting parts of the island.

The funicular drops you just around the corner from Piazza Umberto, the town's main square. With your back to the funicular, the bus stop is 50 yards straight ahead down Via Roma. You'll find the **TI** under the bell tower on Piazza Umberto (for TI details, see "Tourist Information," earlier). The footpath to the port starts just behind the TI, near the baggage storage (follow signs to *Il Porto*, 15-minute walk).

Capri town's multi-domed Baroque **cathedral,** which faces the square, is worth a quick look. (Its multicolored marble floor at the altar was scavenged from the Emperor Tiberius's villa in the 19th century.)

To the left of City Hall (Municipio, lowest corner), a lane leads into the medieval part of town, which has plenty of eateries and is the starting point for the walk to Villa Jovis.

The lane to the left of the cathedral (past Bar Tiberio, under the wide arch) is a fashionable shopping strip that's justifiably been dubbed "Rodeo Drive" by residents. Walk a few minutes down Rodeo Drive (past Gelateria Buonocore at #35, with its tempting fresh waffle cones) to Quisisana Hotel, the island's top old-time hotel. From there, head left for fancy shops and villas, and right for gardens and views. Downhill and to the right, a five-minute walk leads to a lovely public garden, Giardini Augusto, with superb views of the back side of the island (€1, April-Oct daily 9:00-19:30, May and early Nov daily 9:00-17:30, mid-Nov-March shorter hours and free admission, no picnicking).

Villa Jovis and the Emperor's Capri

Even before becoming emperor, Augustus loved Capri so much that he traded the family-owned Isle of Ischia to the (then-independent) Neapolitans in exchange for making Capri his personal property. Emperor Tiberius spent a decade here, A.D. 26-37. (Some figure he did so in order to escape being assassinated in Rome.)

Emperor Tiberius' ruined villa, Villa Jovis, is a scenic 45-minute hike from Capri town. You won't find any statues or mosaics here—just an evocative, ruined complex of terraces fitting a rocky perch over a sheer drop to the sea...and a lovely view. You can make out a large water reservoir for baths, the foundations of servants' quarters, and Tiberius' private apartments (fragments of marble flooring still survive). The ruined lighthouse dates from the Middle Ages.

Cost and Hours: €2, nearly daily 11:00-15:00, closed Tue from 1st to 15th of each month and closed Sun from the 16th to the end of each month, tel. 081-837-4549.

▲▲Blue Grotto

Three thousand tourists a day spend a couple of hours visiting Capri's Blue Grotto (Grotta Azzurra). I did—early (when the light is

best), without the frustration of crowds, and with choppy waves nearly making entrance impossible...and it was great.

The actual cave experience isn't much: a five-minute dinghy ride through a three-foot-high entry hole to reach a 60-yard-long cave, where the sun reflects brilliantly blue on its limestone bottom. But the experience—getting there, getting in, and getting back—is a scenic hoot. You get a fast ride on a 30-foot boat partway around the gorgeous island; along the way you see bird life and dramatic limestone cliffs with scant narration. You'll understand why Roman emperors appreciated the invulnerability of the island—it's surrounded by cliffs, with only one good access point, and therefore easy to defend.

Just outside the grotto, your boat idles as you pile into eight-foot dinghies that hold up to four passengers each. Next, you'll be taken to a floating ticket counter and asked to pass the €12.50 grotto entry fee over the side. From there, your ruffian rower will elbow his way to the tiny hole, then pull fast and hard on the cable at the low point of the swells to squeeze you into the grotto (keep your head down and hands in the boat). Then your man rows you around, spouting off a few descriptive lines and singing "O Sole Mio." Depending upon the strength of the sunshine that day, the blue light inside can be brilliant.

The grotto was actually an ancient Roman *nymphaeum*—a retreat for romantic hanky-panky. Many believe that, in its day, a tunnel led here directly from the palace, and that the grotto experience was enlivened by statues of Poseidon and company, placed half-underwater as if emerging from the sea. It was ancient Romans who smoothed out the entry hole that's still used to this day.

Sometimes, your boatman will try to extort an extra tip out of you before taking you back outside to your big boat (€1 is enough, but you don't need to pay a penny...you've already paid plenty). If you don't want to return by boat, ask your boatman to let you off at the little dock, where stairs lead up to a café and the Blue Grotto bus stop.

Cost: The €12.50 entry fee (separate from the €13.50 ride from Marina Grande) includes €8.50 for the rowboat service plus €4 to cover the admission to the grotto itself. Though signs forbid it, some people dive in for free from the little dock next to the grotto entrance after the boats stop running—a magical experience and a favorite among locals.

Timing: When the waves or high tide make entering dangerous, the boats don't go in—the grotto can close without notice, sending tourists (flush with anticipation) home without a chance to squeeze through the little hole. (If this happens to you, consider the one-hour boat ride around the island offered by both companies.)

If you're coming from Capri's port (Marina Grande), allow 1-3 hours for the entire visit, depending on the chaos at the caves. Going with the first trip will get you there at the same time as the boatmen in their dinghies—who hitch a ride behind your boat—resulting in less chaos and a shorter wait at the entry point.

Getting There: You can either take the boat directly from Marina Grande, as most people do, or save money by taking the bus via Anacapri.

By Boat from Marina Grande: Two companies make the boat trip from different parts of Marina Grande—Laser Capri and Motoscafisti Capri (€13.50 round-trip with either company, no discount for one-way; Motoscafista Capri—tel. 081-837-7714, www.motoscafisticapri.com; Laser Capri—tel. 081-837-5208, www.lasercapri.com). The first boats depart Marina Grande at 9:00, and they continue at least until 13:00—or often later, depending on when the rowboats stop running (likely 17:00 in summer, but earlier off-season).

By Bus via Anacapri: If you're on a budget, you can take the bus from Anacapri to the grotto (rather than a boat from Marina Grande). You'll save about €6 (assuming you take the direct Marina Grande-Anacapri bus and then change to the Anacapri-Blue Grotto bus), lose time, and see a beautiful, calmer side of the island.

Anacapri-Blue Grotto buses (roughly 3/hour, Nov-March 1-2/hour, 10 minutes) depart only from the Anacapri bus station at Piazza della Pace (not from the bus stop at Piazza Vittoria 200 yards away, which is more popular with tourists). If you're coming from Marina Grande or Capri town and want to transfer to the Blue Grotto buses, don't get off when the driver announces "Anacapri." Instead, ride one more stop to Piazza della Pace. If in doubt, ask the driver or a local.

Getting Back from the Blue Grotto: You can either take the boat back, or ask your boatman to drop you off on the small dock next to the grotto entrance, from where you climb up the stairs to the stop for the bus to Anacapri (if you came by boat, you'll still have to pay the full €13.50 round-trip boat fare).

Anacapri

Capri's second town has two or three hours' worth of interesting sights. Though higher up on the island ("ana" means "upper" in Greek), there are no sea views at street level in the town center.

When visiting Anacapri by bus, note that there are two stops: the bus stop by the cemetery (called Piazza della Pace—pronounced "PAH-chay"—though locals may call it by its former name, Piazza del Cimitero), and the more central Piazza Vittoria stop, 200 yards away, by the base of the chairlift to Monte Solaro. It doesn't matter which stop you get off at. But when leaving Anacapri for Capri town or Marina Grande, buses can be packed. Your best chance of getting a seat is to catch the bus from Piazza della Pace, one stop before where most people get on (stand at the street corner under the concrete awning).

Regardless of where you get off, make your way to Via Orlandi, Anacapri's pedestrianized main street. From Piazza della Pace, reach it via the crosswalk and then the small lane called Via Filietto; from Piazza Vittoria, head to the right of the statue of "Anacapri." Anacapri's tiny **TI** is at Via Orlandi 59 (Mon-Sat 9:00-15:00, closed Sun, may be closed Nov-Easter, tel. 081-837-1524, www.capritourism.com).

To see the town, walk on this street for 10 minutes or so. Signs suggest a quick circuit that links the Casa Rossa, St. Michael's Church, and peaceful side streets. You'll also find a number of shops and eateries, including a couple of good choices for quick, inexpensive pizza, *panini,* and other goodies: **Sciué Sciué** (same price for informal seating or take-away, no cover charge, daily April-Oct, closed Nov-March, near the TI at #73, tel. 081-837-2068) and **Pizza e Pasta** (take-away only, daily March-Nov, closed Dec-Feb, just before the church at #157, tel. 328-623-8460).

▲Villa San Michele

This is the 19th-century mansion of Axel Munthe, Capri's grand personality, an idealistic Swedish doctor who lived here until 1943 and whose services to the Swedish royal family brought him into contact with high society. At the very least, walk the path from Piazza Victoria past the villa to a superb, free viewpoint over Capri town and Marina Grande. Paying to enter the villa lets you see a few rooms with a well-done but ho-hum exhibit on Munthe, plus a delightful and extensive garden with a chapel, Olivetum (a tiny museum of native birds and bugs), and a view that's slightly better than the free one outside. A café (also with a view) serves €6 sandwiches. Walking to the villa from Piazza Victoria, you pass the deluxe Capri Palace Hotel—venture in if you can get past the treacherously eye-catching swimming pool windows.

Cost and Hours: €7, May-Sept daily 9:00-18:00, closes earlier Oct-April, last entry 20 minutes before closing, tel. 081-837-1401, www.villasanmichele.eu.

Casa Rossa (Red House)

This "Pompeiian-red," eccentric home, a hodgepodge of architectural styles, is the former residence of John Clay MacKowen, a Louisiana doctor and ex-Confederate officer who moved to Capri in the 1870s and married a local girl. (MacKowen and Axel Munthe loathed each other, and even tried to challenge each other to a duel.) Its small collection of 19th-century paintings of scenes from around the island recalls a time before mass tourism. Don't miss the second floor, with its four ancient, sea-worn statues, which were recovered from the depths of the Blue Grotto in the 1960s and '70s.

Cost and Hours: €3; free with ticket stub from Blue Grotto, Villa San Michele, or Monte Solaro chairlift; June-Sept Tue-Sun 10:00-13:30 & 17:30-20:00, closed Mon; April-May Tue-Sun 10:00-17:00, closed Mon; Oct Tue-Sun 10:00-16:00, closed Mon; closed Nov-March, Via Orlandi 78, tel. 081-838-2193.

▲Church of San Michele

This Baroque church in the village center has a remarkable majolica floor showing paradise on earth in a classic 18th-century Neapolitan style. The entire floor is ornately tiled, featuring an angel (with flaming sword) driving Adam and Eve from paradise. The devil is wrapped around the trunk of a beautiful tree. The animals—happily ignoring this momentous event—all have human expressions. For the best view, climb the spiral stairs from the postcard desk. Services are held only during the first two weeks of Advent, when the church is closed to visitors.

Cost and Hours: €2, daily April-Oct 9:00-19:00, Nov and mid-Dec-March 10:00-14:00, closed late Nov-mid Dec, in town center just off Via Orlandi—look for signs for *San Michele,* tel. 081-837-2396, www.chiesa-san-michele.com.

Faro

The lighthouse is a favorite place to enjoy the sunset, with a private beach, pool, small restaurants, and a few fishermen. Reach it by bus from Anacapri (3/hour, departs from Piazza della Pace stop).

▲▲Chairlift up to Monte Solaro

From Anacapri, ride the chairlift *(seggiovia)* to the 1,900-foot summit of Monte Solaro for a commanding view of the Bay of Naples.

Work on your tan as you float over hazelnut, walnut, chestnut, apricot, peach, kiwi, and fig trees, past a montage of tourists (mostly from cruise ships; when the grotto is closed—as it often is—they bring passengers here instead). Prospective smoochers should know that the lift seats are all single. As you ascend, consider how Capri's real estate has been priced out of the locals' reach. The ride takes 13 minutes each way, and you'll want at least 30 minutes on top, where there are picnic benches and a cafe with WCs.

Cost and Hours: €7.50 one-way, €10 round-trip, daily June-Oct 9:30-17:00, last run down at 17:30, closes earlier Nov-May, confirm schedule with TI, departs from top of the steps in Piazza Vittoria—the first Anacapri bus stop, tel. 081-837-1428, www.seggioviamontesolaro.it.

At the Summit: You'll enjoy the best panorama possible: lush cliffs busy with seagulls enjoying the ideal nesting spot. Find the Faraglioni Rocks—with tour boats squeezing through every few minutes—which are an icon of the island. The pink building nearest the rocks was an American R&R base during World War II. Eisenhower and Churchill met here. On the peak closest to Cape Sorrento, you can see the distant ruins of the Emperor Tiberius' palace, Villa Jovis. Pipes from the Sorrento Peninsula bring water to Capri (demand for fresh water here long ago exceeded the supply provided by the island's three natural springs). The Galli Islands mark the Amalfi Coast in the distance. Cross the bar terrace for views of Mount Vesuvius and Naples.

Hiking Down: A highlight for hardy walkers (provided you have strong knees and good shoes) is the 40-minute downhill hike from the top of Monte Solaro, through lush vegetation and ever-changing views, past the 14th-century Chapel of Santa Maria Cetrella (at the trail's only intersection, it's a 10-minute detour to the right), and back into Anacapri. The trail starts downstairs, past the WCs (last chance). Down two more flights of stairs, look for the sign to *Anacapri e Cetrella*—you're on your way. While the trail is well-established, you'll encounter plenty of uneven steps, loose rocks, and few signs.

SORRENTO & CAPRI

Capri Connections

From Capri's Marina Grande by Boat to: Sorrento (fast ferry: 4/day, 25 minutes, €13; hydrofoil: up to 20/day, 20 minutes, €16-17), **Naples** (1-2/hour, hydrofoil: 50 minutes, €18-19; ferries: 60-80 minutes, €11-16); **Positano** (mid-April-mid-Oct, 2-4/day, 30-60 minutes, €17-19; less off-season), **Amalfi** (mid-April-mid-Oct, 1/day, 1.5 hours, €19). Confirm the schedule carefully at TIs or www.capritourism.org—last boats usually leave between 18:00 and 20:10.

AMALFI COAST AND PAESTUM

With its stunning scenery, hill- and harbor-hugging towns, and historic ruins, Amalfi is Italy's coast with the most. The bus trip from Sorrento to Salerno along the breathtaking Amalfi Coast is one of the world's great bus rides. It will leave your mouth open and your camera's memory card full. You'll gain respect for the 19th-century Italian engineers who built the roads—and even more respect for the 21st-century bus drivers who drive it. Cantilevered garages, hotels, and villas cling to the vertical terrain, and beautiful sandy coves tease from far below and out of reach. As you hyperventilate, notice how the Mediterranean, a sheer 500-foot drop below, really twinkles. All this beautiful scenery apparently inspires local Romeos and Juliets, with the latex evidence of late-night romantic encounters littering the roadside turnouts. Over the centuries, the spectacular scenery and climate have been a siren call for the rich and famous, luring Roman emperor Tiberius, Richard Wagner, Sophia Loren, Gore Vidal, and others to the Amalfi Coast's special brand of *la dolce vita*.

Amalfi Coast towns are pretty, but they're generally touristy, congested, overpriced, and a long hike above tiny, pebbly beaches. (For that reason, many visitors prefer side-tripping in from Sorrento.) Most beaches here are private, and access is expensive. Check and understand your bills in this greedy region.

Planning Your Time

On a quick visit, use Sorrento (described in the previous chapter) as your home base and do the Amalfi Coast as a day trip. But for a small-town vacation from your vacation, spend a few more days on the coast, perhaps sleeping in Positano or Amalfi town.

Getting Around the Amalfi Coast

Trying to decide between staying in Sorrento, Positano, or Amalfi? Sorrento is the largest of the three, with useful services and the best transportation connections and accommodations. Positano is the most chic and picturesque, with a decent beach, but tiny and expensive. The town of Amalfi has the most actual sights and the best hiking opportunities, but lacks good-value places to stay.

Getting Around the Amalfi Coast

The real thrill here is the scenic Amalfi drive. This is treacherous stuff—even if you have a car, you may want to take the bus or hire a taxi. Brave souls enjoy seeing the coast by scooter or motorbike (rent in Sorrento). The most logical springboard for this trip is Sorrento, but Positano and Amalfi work, too.

Below, I've outlined your options by bus, boat, and taxi. Many travelers do the Amalfi Coast as a round-trip by bus, but a good strategy is to go one way by bus and return by boat. For example, instead of busing from Sorrento to Salerno (end of the line) and back, consider taking the bus to Salerno, then catching the ferry back to Amalfi or Positano, and then, from either town, hopping another ferry to Sorrento. Perhaps the simplest option is to take the bus to Positano and boat from there back to Sorrento (or vice versa). Note that ferries run less often in spring and fall, and some don't run at all off-season (mid-Oct-mid-April). Boats don't run in stormy weather at any time of year.

Looking for exercise? Consider an Amalfi Coast hike. Numerous trails connect the main towns along the coast with villages on the hills. Get a good map and/or book before you venture out.

By Bus

From Sorrento: SITA buses depart from Sorrento's train station nearly hourly (in peak season, 20/day, marked *Amalfi via Positano*) and stop at all Amalfi Coast towns (Positano in 50 minutes; Amalfi in another 50 minutes). To reach Salerno (3 hours), at the far end of the coast, you have to transfer in Amalfi. Ticket prices vary with trip length (45-minute ride, good for short hops-€2.50; 1.5-hour ride, good from Sorrento to Positano-€3.80; 24-hour day pass, good to Amalfi and beyond-€7.60; 3-day ticket-€18). For most trips, you'll want the 24-hour day pass.

In summer, buses start running as early as 6:30 and run as late as 22:00 (they stop running earlier off-season; check the schedule). Buy tickets at the tobacco shop nearest any bus stop before boarding.

An info booth is across from the bus stop at the Sorrento train station (mid-April-Oct daily 8:30-13:30), but the tobacco shop/newsstand at street level inside the station is more reliable (daily 7:00-13:30 & 14:30-20:00, also sells Circumvesuviana train tickets). If both are closed, try the appropriately named Snack Bar, upstairs in the station, or Bar Frisby, just down the hill.

Line up under the *Bus Stop SITA* sign (where a schedule is posted on the wall) across from the Sorrento train station (10 steps down). Carefully note the lettered codes that differentiate daily buses from weekend-only buses. *Giornaliero* means daily; *Feriale* denotes Monday-Saturday departures; and *Festivo* is for Sundays and holidays. After 19:30 (and occasionally on Sundays—check the sign at the main bus stop), buses may leave from Via degli Aranci (with your back to the station, go left and wind around it; the bus stop is near Bar Paradise).

Leaving Sorrento, grab a seat on the right for the best views. If you return by bus, it's fun to sit directly behind the driver for a box seat with a view over the twisting hairpin action. Sitting toward the front will also help minimize carsickness.

Avoiding Crowds on the Bus: Amalfi Coast buses are routinely unable to handle the demand during summer months and holidays. Occasionally, an extra bus is added to deal with the overflow. Generally, if you don't get on one bus, you're well-positioned to catch the next one (bring a book). Try to arrive early in the morning. Remember that buses start taking off as early as 6:30; beginning at 8:30, they leave about every 30 minutes. Departures between 9:00 and 11:00 are crowded and frustrating. Count the number of people in line: Buses pull into Sorrento empty and seat 48 (plus 25 standing). Remember that an eight-seater minibus and driver costs about €300 for the day—if you can organize a small group, €40 per person is a very good deal.

Returning to Sorrento: The congestion can be so bad in the summer—particularly July and August—that return buses don't even stop in Positano (because they've been filled in Amalfi). Those trying to get back to Sorrento are stuck with taking an extortionist taxi or, if in Positano, hopping a boat...if one's running. If touring the coast by bus, do Positano first and come home from Amalfi to avoid the problem of full buses.

By Boat

Several companies compete for passengers, and usually claim to know nothing about their rivals' services. It's wise to check posted schedules, pick up ferry schedules from the TI, and confirm times to figure out the best plan. Boats stop at Sorrento, Positano, Amalfi, and Salerno, generally from mid-April through mid-October (pick up schedule at TI, buy ticket on dock). Few boats run off-season.

By Taxi

Given the hairy driving, impossible parking, congested buses, and potential fun, you might consider splurging to hire your own car and driver for the Amalfi day. (Don't bother for Pompeii, as the Circumvesuviana train serves it conveniently and only licensed guides can take you into the site.)

The Monetti family car-and-driver service—Raffaele, brother-in-law Tony, and cousin Lorenzo—have long taken excellent care of my readers' transit needs from Sorrento. Sample trips and rates: all-day Amalfi Coast (Positano, Amalfi, Ravello), eight hours, €280; Amalfi Coast and Paestum, 10 hours, €400; transfer to Naples airport or train station to Sorrento, €110 (these prices are for up to three people, more for a larger eight-seater van). Though Sorrento-based, they also do trips from Naples (more expensive). Payment is by cash only. Their reservation system is simple and reliable (Raffaele's mobile 335-602-9158 or 338-946-2860, "office" run by his English-speaking Finnish wife, Susanna, www.monettitaxi17.it, monettitaxi17@libero.it). Don't just hop into any taxi claiming to be a Monetti—call first. If you get into any kind of a serious jam in the area, you can call Raffaele for help.

Francesco del Pizzo is another smooth and honest driver. A classy young man who speaks English well, Francesco enjoys explaining things as he drives (nine hours or so in a car with up to four passengers, €280; up to eight passengers in a minibus, €320; mobile 333-238-4144, francescodelpizzo@yahoo.it).

Umberto and Giovanni Benvenuto offer transport, narrated tours, and shore excursions throughout the Amalfi Coast, as well as to Rome, Naples, Pompeii, and more. They are based in Praiano (near Positano). While as friendly as the Monettis, they're more upmarket and formal, with steeper rates explained on their website (tel. 081-007-2114, mobile 346-684-0226, US tel. 310-424-5640, www.benvenutolimos.com, info@benvenutolimos.com).

Sorrento Silver Star, with professional drivers and comfortable Mercedes cars and vans, offers custom trips throughout the area at prices between the Monettis' and Benvenutos' (tel. 081-877-1224, mobile 339-388-8143, www.sorrentosilverstar.com, luisa@sorrentosilverstar.com, Luisa).

Anthony Buonocore is based in Amalfi but does excursions and transfers anywhere in the region in his eight-person Mercedes van (rates vary depending on trip, tel. 349-441-0336, www.amalfitransfer.com, buonocoreanthony@yahoo.it).

Rides Only: If you're hiring a cabbie off the street for a ride and not a tour, here are sample fares from Sorrento to Positano: up to four people one-way for about €80 in a car, or up to six people for €90 in a minibus. Figure on paying 50 percent more to Amalfi. While taxis must use a meter within a city, a fixed rate is OK otherwise. Negotiate—ask about a round-trip.

By Tour

While hiring your own driver is convenient, it's also expensive. To bring the cost down, split the trip—and the bill—with other travelers using this book. Naples-based **Mondo Tour** offers an all-day, nine-hour, lightly guided minibus trip that departs from Sorrento and heads down the Amalfi Coast, with stops in Positano, Amalfi,

AMALFI COAST

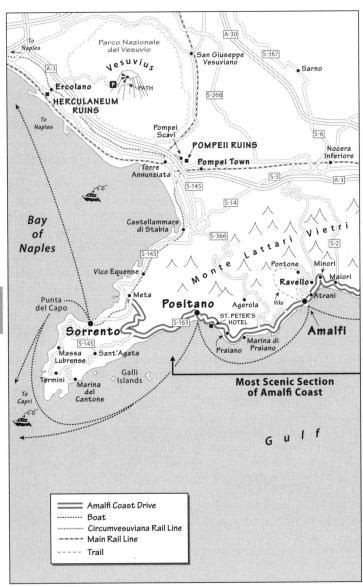

Legend:
- Amalfi Coast Drive
- Boat
- Circumvesuviana Rail Line
- Main Rail Line
- Trail

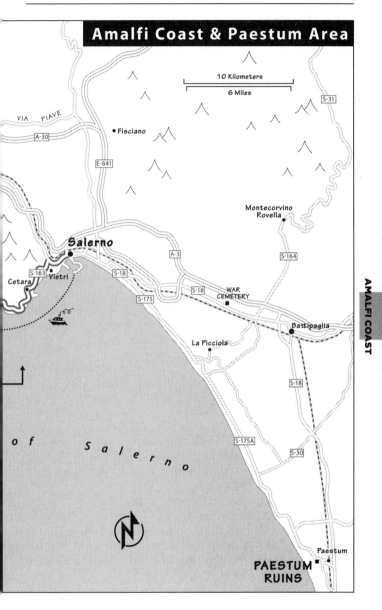

Amalfi Coast & Paestum Area

10 Kilometers

6 Miles

S-31

VIA PIAVE

A-30

• Fisciano

E-841

Montecorvino Rovella

Salerno

A-3

S-164

S-163

Vietri

S-18

Cetara

S-175

S-18

WAR CEMETERY

S-18

Battipaglia

La Picciola

of *Salerno*

S-18

S-175A

S-30

Paestum

PAESTUM RUINS

AMALFI COAST

and Ravello, before returning to Sorrento (€45/person). They also offer Rick Steves readers shared tours in Pompeii and in Naples.

Self-Guided Bus Tour

Hugging the Amalfi Coast

The trip from Sorrento to Salerno is one of the all-time great white-knuckle rides. Gasp from the right side of the bus as you go out and from the left as you return to Sorrento. (Those on the wrong side really miss out.) Traffic is so heavy that private tour buses are only allowed to go in one direction (southbound from Sorrento)—summer traffic is infuriating. Fluorescent-vested policemen are posted at tough bends during peak hours to help fold in side-view mirrors and keep things moving.

Here's a loosely guided tour of what you're seeing, from west to east (note that many of these towns are described in greater detail later in this chapter):

Leaving Sorrento, the road winds up into the hills past lemon groves and hidden houses. Traveling the coast, you'll see several watchtowers placed within sight of each other, so that a relay of rooftop bonfires could spread word of a Saracen (Turkish pirate) attack. The gray-green trees are olives. Dark, green-leafed trees planted in dense groves are the source of the region's lemons—many destined to become *limoncello* liqueur. The black nets over the orange and lemon groves create a greenhouse effect, trapping warmth and humidity for maximum tastiness, while offering protection from extreme weather (preserving the peels used for *limoncello*).

Atop the ridge outside of Sorrento, look to your right: The two small islands after Sorrento are the **Li Galli Islands**; the bigger one, on the left, is Ulysses Island. These islands, once owned by the famed ballet dancer Rudolf Nureyev, mark the boundary between the Bay of Naples and the Bay of Salerno. Technically, the Amalfi Coast drive begins here.

The limestone cliffs that plunge into the sea were traversed by an ancient trail that became a modern road in the mid-19th century. Fruit stands sell produce from farms and orchards just over the hill. Limestone absorbs the heat and rainwater, making this south-facing coastline a fertile suntrap, with temperatures as much as 10 degrees higher than in nearby Sorrento. Bougainvillea and geraniums grow like weeds here in the summer. Notice the nets—they're designed to catch rocks that often tumble loose after absorbing heavy rains.

As you approach the exotic-looking town of **Positano,** you know you've reached the scenic heart of the Amalfi Coast. Views of Positano, the main stop along the coast, are dramatic on either side of town. Just south of Positano, **St. Peter's Hotel** (Il San Pietro di Positano, camouflaged below the tiny St. Peter's church) is just about the most posh stop on the coast. Notice the elevator to the beach and dock. **Praiano** is notable for its cathedral, with the characteristic majolica-tiled roof and dome—a reminder of this region's respected ceramics industry. It's a spindly town, with most of its homes accessible only by tiny footpaths and staircases. Just past the tunnel stands another Saracen watchtower.

Marina di Praiano is a tiny and unique fishing hamlet wedged into a tight ravine with a couple of restaurants and some small ho-

tels.

The next Saracen tower guarded the harbor of the Amalfi navy until the fleet was destroyed in 1343 by a tsunami caused by an earthquake.

The most striking stretch of coastline ends at **Amalfi** and **Atrani.** As you leave Amalfi, look up to the left. The white house that clings to a cliff (Villa Rondinaia) was home for many years to the writer Gore Vidal. Atop the cliff is the town of **Ravello.** From here, the western half of the Amalfi Coast is mostly wild and unpopulated until you hit **Salerno,** and, farther south, the striking Greek temples at **Paestum.**

AMALFI COAST

Positano

According to legend, the Greek god Poseidon created Positano for Pasitea, a nymph he lusted after. History says the town was found-ed when ancient Greeks at Paestum decided to move out of the swamp (to escape the malaria carried by its mosquitoes). Specializing in scenery and sand, Positano hangs half-way between Sorrento and Amalfi town on the most spectacular stretch of the coast.

In antiquity, Positano was famed for its bold sailors and hearty fleet. But after a big 1343 tsunami and the pirate raids of the Middle Ages, its wealth and power declined. It flourished again as a favorite under the Bourbon royal family in the 1700s, when many of its fine mansions were built. Until the late 1800s, the only access was by donkey path or by sea. In the 20th century, Positano became a haven for artists and writers escaping Communist Russia or Nazi Germany. In 1953, American writer John Steinbeck's essay on the town popularized Positano among tourists, and soon after it became a trendy Riviera stop. That was when the town gave the world "Moda Positano"—a leisurely *dolce vita* lifestyle of walking barefoot; wearing bright, happy, colorful clothes; and sporting skimpy bikinis.

Today, the village, a breathtaking sight from a distance, is a pleasant gathering of cafés and expensive stores, with a good but pebbly beach. Positano is famous for its fashions—90 percent of its shops are women's clothing boutiques.

The "skyline" looks like it did a century ago. Notice the town's characteristic Saracen-inspired rooftop domes. Filled with sand, these provide low-tech insulation—to help buildings in the days before air-conditioning stay cool in summer and warm in winter. Traditionally, they were painted white in summer and black in winter.

It's been practically impossible to get a building permit in Positano for over 25 years now, and landowners who want to renovate can't make external changes. The steep stairs are a way of life for the 4,000 hardy locals. Only one street in Positano allows motorized traffic; the rest are steep pedestrian lanes. Because hotels don't take large groups (bus access is too difficult), this town—unlike Sorrento—has been spared the ravages of big-bus tourism.

Consider seeing Positano as a day trip from Sorrento: Take the bus out and the afternoon ferry home, but be sure to check the boat schedules when you arrive—the last ferry often leaves before 18:00, and doesn't always run in spring and fall. Or spend the night to enjoy the magic of Positano. The town has a local flavor at night, when the grown-ups stroll and the kids play soccer on the church porch.

Orientation to Positano

Squished into a ravine, with narrow alleys that cascade down to the harbor, Positano requires you to stroll, whether you're going up or heading down. The center of town has no main square (unless you count the beach). There's little to do here but eat, window-shop, and enjoy the beach and views...hence the town's popularity.

Tourist Information

The TI—which feels pulled out of a classic old Italian movie—is a half-block from the beach, in a small building at the bottom of the church steps (April-Sept Mon-Sat 8:30-19:00, Sun 9:00-14:00; Oct-March Mon-Sat 9:00-16:30, closed Sun; Via del Saracino 4, tel. 089-875-067, www.aziendaturismopositano.it).

Arrival in Positano

The main coast highway winds above the town. Regional SITA buses (blue or green-and-white) stop at two scheduled bus stops located at either end of town: Chiesa Nuova (at Bar Internazionale, near the Sorrento end of town; use this one only if you're staying at Brikette Hostel) and Sponda (nearer Amalfi town). Although both stops are near roads leading downhill through the town to the beach, Sponda is closer and less steep; from this stop, it's a 20-minute downhill stroll/shop/munch to the beach (and TI).

Neither bus stop has **baggage storage**, which makes it hard to visit Positano on the way (for example, between overnights in Sorrento and Amalfi). Your best bet is to get off at Chiesa Nuova and head for the Brikette Hostel, which offers day privileges for €10, including luggage storage, Wi-Fi, and showers. A last resort would be to get off at the Sponda stop and roll your bags all the way down to Piazza dei Mulini, where Positano's porters tend to hang out. They're usually willing to mind your luggage for €5/bag.

If you're catching the SITA bus back to Sorrento, be aware that it may leave from the Sponda stop up to five minutes before the printed departure. There's simply no room for the bus to wait, so in case the driver is early, you should be, too (€3.80, departures about hourly, daily 7:00-22:00, until 20:00 off-season). Buy tickets from the tobacco shop next to Bar Mulino Verde in the town center, or just below the Sponda bus stop at the Li Galli Bar or Total gas station (across from Hotel Marincanto).

If the walk up to the stop is too tough, take the dizzy little local red-and-white shuttle bus (marked *Interno Positano*), which constantly loops through Positano, connecting the lower town with the highway's two bus stops (2/hour, €1.20 at tobacco shop or €1.50 on board, catch it at convenient stop at the corner of Via Colombo and Via dei Mulini, heads up to Sponda). Bar Mulino Verde, located off Piazza dei Mulini (as close as cars, taxis, and the shuttle bus can get to the beach), is just across from the shuttle bus stop, with a fine, breezy terrace you can enjoy if you're waiting.

Drivers must go with the one-way flow, entering the town only at the Chiesa Nuova bus stop (closest to Sorrento) and exiting at Sponda. Driving is a headache here. Parking is even worse.

AMALFI COAST

Tours in Positano

Local Guide

Christine Ornelas, an Australian lawyer who fell for a local and married into the Positano scene, has become the town historian. She weaves her interests into a fascinating three-hour walk through town. Christine's tour gives the town context and brings meaning to fun hidden history, while offering an overview of the local scene, tastings of local products, and tips on shopping, beaches, restaurants, and excursions (€25, 2 people-€45 with this book, April–mid-Nov daily at 10:30, email or call to confirm—she'll do the tour for even just a couple of people, mobile 334-232-2096, www. discoverpositano.it, christineornelas@gmail.com). Christine's walk starts at Piazza dei Mulini (outside the church, Chiesa del Rosario).

Self-Guided Walk

Welcome to Positano

While there's no real sightseeing in Positano, this short, guided stroll downhill will help you get your bearings from top to bottom.

• Start at...

Piazza dei Mulini: This is the upper-town meeting point—as close to the beach as vehicles can get—and is also the lower stop for the little red-and-white shuttle bus (2/hour, departs on the hour and half-hour). Bar Mulino Verde is *the* local hangout—older people gather inside, while the younger crowd congregates on the wisteria-draped terrace across the street. In this small town, gossiping is a big pastime.

Positano's ceramic and linen industries boomed when tourists discovered the place in the 1970s. The beach-inspired Moda Positano fashion label was first created as a break from the rigid dress code of the '50s. On this piazza, and throughout town, you'll find lots of ceramic and linen shops (and an abundance of ATMs), along with galleries featuring the work of local artists.

• *Wander downhill to the "fork" in the road (stairs to the left, road to the right). You've reached...*

Midtown: At Enoteca Cuomo (#3), butcher Vincenzo stocks fine local red wines and is happy to explain their virtues. He also makes homemade sausages, salami, and *panini*—good for a quick lunch. The smaller set of stairs leads to the recommended Delicatessen grocery store, where Emilia can fix you a good picnic (see "Eating in Positano," later). Their downstairs café (enter past the stairs, on the left at #13) sells an array of tempting lemon candies and other edible souvenirs.

La Zagara (across the lane at #10) is a pastry shop by day and a piano bar by night. Tempting pastries such as the rum-drenched *babà* (a southern Italian favorite) fill the window display. After hours, it's filled with traditional Neapolitan music and dancing. A bit farther downhill, Brunella (#24) is respected for traditional, quality, and locally made linens.

Across the street, Hotel Palazzo Murat fills what was once a grand Benedictine monastery. Step into the plush courtyard to enjoy the scene. Continuing on, under a fragrant bougainvillea trellis, you'll come to "street merchants' gulch," where artisans display their goodies.

• *Continue under the bougainvillea trellis, turning right at the church, and go downstairs to Piazza Flavio Gioia, with the big...*

Church of Santa Maria Assunta: This church originated as the abbey of Positano's 12th-century Benedictine monastery. Originally Romanesque, it was eventually abandoned (along with the entire lower town) out of fear of pirate attacks. When the coast was clear in the 18th century, the church was given an extreme Baroque makeover. Its dome is covered in colorful majolica tiles.

Inside (first chapel on left) is a fine manger scene *(presepe)*. Its original 18th-century figurines give you an idea of the folk costumes of the age. Above the main altar is the Black Madonna, an icon-like Byzantine painting, which was likely brought here in the 12th century by Benedictine monks. But locals prefer the romantic legend: Saracen pirates had it on their ship as plunder. A violent storm hit—sure to sink the evil ship. The painting of Mary spoke, saying, *"Posa, posa"* (lay me down), and the ship glided safely to this harbor. The pirates were so stricken they became Christians. Locals kept the painting, and the town became known as *Posatano* (recalling Mary's command). To the right of the altar, a small chapel holds a silver and copper bust of St. Vitus—the town patron who brought Christianity here in about A.D. 300 (this may be displayed nearby in a freestanding wooden altar). In the adjacent niche (on the right) is a rare 1599 painting by Fabrizio Santafede of Baby Jesus being circumcised, considered the finest historic painting in town.

Back outside, you'll see the bell tower, dating from 1707. Above the door, it sports a Romanesque relief scavenged from the original church. The scene—a wolf mermaid with seven little fish—was a reminder to worshippers of how integral the sea was to their livelihood. Notice the characteristic shallow, white "insulation domes" on rooftops in front of the church.

• *Backtrack up the steps, circling around the church until you see an information board labeled* Villa Romana.

The information board describes, in English, how this spot once held a Roman villa, buried when Mount Vesuvius erupted in A.D. 79. Only a few minor rooms have been excavated (a photograph shows one of the preserved frescoes). The rest await discovery—digging has ceased until there are enough funds to do it properly. The stairs lead down to two glass doors that would (if this very rich town could afford to keep them open) offer a peek into the church's crypt—originally the early church's altar. According to local legend, the Benedictines sat their dead brothers on the stone choir chairs here to decompose and remind all of their mortality.

• *Continue climbing down the steps arcing to the right. You'll eventually come to the little square, with concrete benches, facing the beach.*

Piazzetta: This is the local gathering point in the evening, as local boys hustle tourist girls into the nearby nightclub. Residents traded their historic baptistery font with Amalfi town for the two iron lions you see facing the beach. From here, you can look up and admire the colorful majolica tiles so typical of church domes in this region. Positano was once a notable naval power, with many shipyards along this beach. These eventually became fishermen's quarters and storehouses, and later, today's tourist restaurants. The Positano **beach,** called Spiaggia Grande, is half public (with WC and €1 shower) and half private.

• *On the far left side of the beach is...*

Music on the Rocks: This chic, recommended club (below the Ristorante e Terrazze) is all that's left of the 1970s scene, when Positano really rocked. While it's dead until about 23:00, if you just want to stop for a drink, the cool troglo-disco interior opens at 21:00.

• *Wander across the beach. Beyond the kiosks that sell boat tickets, a path climbs up and over, past a 13th-century lookout fort from Saracen pirate days, to the next beach. It's a worthwhile little five-minute walk to...*

Fornillo Beach: This is where locals go for better swimming and to escape some of the tourist crowds. The walk over offers a welcome change of scene, as the path winds through a shady ravine.

• *Our walk is over. Time to relax.*

Sights in Positano

Beaches

Positano's pebbly and sandy primary beach, **Spiaggia Grande,** is colorful with umbrellas as it stretches wide around the cove. It's mostly private (€10-15/person, April-Oct, cost includes drink service and use of lounge chair and umbrella), with a free section near the middle, close to where the boats take off. The nearest WC is beneath the steps to the right (as you face the water).

Fornillo Beach, a less-crowded option just around the bend (to the west) of Spiaggia Grande, is favored by residents, with more affordable chair and umbrella rentals. This beach has a few humble snack bars and lunch eateries.

Boat Trips

At the west end of Spiaggia Grande (to the right as you face the sea), booths sell tickets to a number of destinations. Consider renting a rowboat or taking a boat tour to a nearby cave (La Grotta dello Smeraldo—Emerald Cave), fishing village (Nerano), or small islands.

Ferries run to Amalfi, Capri, and Sorrento.

Shopping

Locally produced linens and ceramics can be found at shops and galleries throughout town. **Ceramica Assunta,** one of the oldest ceramics stores in Positano, carries colorful Solimene dinnerware and more at two locations (Via Colombo 97 and Via Colombo 137, tel. 089-875-008). The young owner-artisan couple at **Sunflower Bottega d'Arte** make and paint their own ceramic designs. Two popular (and pricey) fashion boutiques are **Brunella** (Via Pasitea 72, tel. 089-875-228) and **Pepito's** (Via Pasitea 39, tel. 089-875-446).

Nightlife

The big-time action in the old town center is the impressive club **Music on the Rocks,** literally carved into the rocks on the beach (opens at 21:00 mid-April-Oct but party starts about 23:30, on summer weekends often a €10-20 cover charge that includes a drink, go to dance or just check out the scene, Via Grotte Dell'Incanto 51, tel. 089-875-874, www.musicontherocks.it). For a more low-key atmosphere, café/pastry shop **La Zagara** hosts music nightly in summer (June-Sept, starts around 21:00, Via dei Mulini 10, tel. 089-875-964).

Sleeping in Positano

These hotels (but not the hostel) are all on or near Via Colombo, which leads from the SITA Sponda bus stop down into the village. Prices given are for the highest season (May-Sept)—at other times, they become soft. Most places close in the winter (Dec-Feb or longer). Expect to pay more than €20 a day to park, except at Albergo California.

$$$ Hotel Marincanto is a recently restored, somewhat impersonal four-star hotel with 32 beautiful rooms and a bright breakfast terrace practically teetering on a cliff. Suites seem to be designed for a *luna di miele*—honeymoon (Db-€220, more expen-

Sleep Code

(€1 = about $1.30, country code: 39)

S = Single, **D** = Double/Twin, **T** = Triple, **Q** = Quad, **b** = bathroom, **s** = shower only. Unless otherwise noted, credit cards are accepted, English is spoken, and breakfast is included. Many towns in Italy levy a hotel tax of €2 per person, per night, which must be paid in cash (not included in the rates I've quoted).

To help you sort easily through these listings, I've divided the accommodations into three categories based on the price for a standard double room with bath:

$$$ **Higher Priced**—Most rooms €180 or more.

$$ **Moderately Priced**—Most rooms between €130-180.

$ **Lower Priced**—Most rooms €130 or less.

Prices can change without notice; verify the hotel's current rates online or by email. For the best prices, always book direct.

sive superior rooms and suites, extra bed-€70, air-con, elevator, guest computer, free Wi-Fi, pool, private stairs to beach, parking-€26/day, closed Nov-March, 50 yards below Sponda bus stop at Via Colombo 50, reception on bottom floor, tel. 089-875-130, www.marincanto.it, info@marincanto.it).

$$ Hotel Savoia is family-run, with 39 sizeable, breezy, bright, simple rooms with tiles and older furnishings (viewless Db-€120, view Db-€170, deluxe Db with balcony or terrace-€200, at least €10/day less with this book in 2014, extra bed-€50, air-con, elevator, free Wi-Fi in common areas, closed Nov-Feb, Via Colombo 73, tel. 089-875-003, www.savoiapositano.it, info@savoiapositano.it, Regina and daughters Mechy, Piera, and Cristina).

$$ Hotel Bougainville rents 16 comfortable rooms, half with balconies. Everything's bright, modern, and tasteful (small-windowed viewless economy Db-€119, regular viewless Db-€140, view Db-€185, 5 percent off these rates if you book direct with this book in 2014, check website for specials, air-con, guest computer, free Wi-Fi, closed Nov-March, Via Colombo 25, tel. 089-875-047, www.bougainville.it, info@bougainville.it, friendly Marella).

$$ Albergo California has 15 spacious rooms (all with lofty views), a grand terrace draped with vines, and full breakfasts. The Cinque family—including Maria, Bronx-born son John, and grandson Giuseppe—will welcome you (view Db-€160 June-Sept, €10 less April-May and Oct, these prices promised with this book through 2014, air-con, Wi-Fi, free parking, closed Nov-March,

Via Colombo 141, tel. 089-875-382, www.hotelcaliforniapositano. it, info@hotelcaliforniapositano.it).

$ Hotel Pupetto is a family-run hotel for beach lovers. This secluded waterfront spot is a 10-minute walk from Positano's bustling harbor (Db-€95-120, Via Fornillo 37, tel. 089-875-087, www.hotelpupetto.it, info@hotelpupetto.it).

$ Residence la Tavolozza is an attractive six-room hotel, warmly run by Celeste (cheh-LEHS-tay) and daughters Francesca (who speaks English) and Paola. Each cheerily tiled room comes with a view, a terrace, and silence. This is a good value (Db-€95-120 depending on size, doesn't include breakfast, these prices promised through 2014 with this book, families can ask for sprawling "Royal Apartment"—price varies depending on occupancy, call to confirm if arriving late, extra for lavish à la carte breakfast, air-con, free Wi-Fi, closed Dec-Feb, Via Colombo 10, tel. 089-875-040, www. latavolozzapositano.it).

$ Brikette Hostel offers your best cheap dorm-bed option in this otherwise ritzy town. Renting 35 beds and offering a great sun and breakfast terrace, it has a loose, youthful, rough-around-the-edges ambience (bunk in humble 10-bed dorm-€25, bunk in 8-bed dorm-€28, bunk in 5-bed dorm-€33, Db-€90, nicer Db-€120, bigger family rooms; hearty breakfast-€5, €5-7 dinners; air-con in a few rooms, free Wi-Fi; day privileges for day-trippers, including luggage storage-€10; 11:00-14:30 lockout for cleaning, closed mid-Nov-March, leave bus at Chiesa Nuova/Bar Internazionale stop and backtrack uphill 500 feet to Via G. Marconi 358, tel. 089-875-857, www.hostel-positano.com, hostelpositano@gmail.com).

Eating in Positano

Positano is an expensive place to dine. At the waterfront, several interchangeable restaurants with view terraces leave people fat and happy, albeit with skinnier wallets (figure €15-20 pastas and *secondi*, plus pricey drinks and sides, and a cover charge). Little distinguishes one place from the next; all are pleasant, convenient, and over-priced.

"Uptown": The unassuming, family-run **Ristorante Bruno** is handy to my listed hotels. Consider it if you want an expensive meal without hiking down into the town center for dinner (€12-16 pastas, €16-22 *secondi*, daily 12:00-23:00, closed Nov-Easter, near the top of Via Colombo at #157, tel. 089-875-179).

AMALFI COAST

"Way Uptown": **Ristorante Scirocco** is a splurge, perched high above Positano with fantastic views and meals ranging from seafood to steak. Get there with enough daylight left to enjoy the scenery. New owners may mean changes to the menu or pricing in 2014 (€12 pastas, €18 *secondi*, €35 fixed-price meal, daily 12:00-15:00 & 19:00-24:00, closed Nov-Easter, Via Montepertuso 126, tel. 089-875-184).

Inexpensive Pizza & Pasta: **Capricci,** three doors from the TI, is budget-priced (for Positano). An informal café and *tavola calda* serves up €7.50 pizza and €8.50 main courses that you can eat on the spot or take away. If you sit down at their white-tablecloth restaurant across the street, you get the same food—but the pizza price jumps to €10, with a €2 cover (daily 9:00-23:00, Via Regina Giovanna 12, tel. 089-812-145). They deliver anywhere in Positano during slow hours for €3 (Tue-Sun 9:00-11:30 & 16:00-19:00, no delivery at other times or on Mon, menu at www.capriccipositano.it).

Picnics: If a picnic dinner on your balcony or the beach sounds good, sunny Emilia at the **Delicatessen** grocery store can supply the ingredients (*antipasto misto* to go at €1.40/100 grams, pasta for €1/100 grams, sandwiches made and sold by weight—about €3.50-4.50, she microwaves food and includes all the picnic ware, come early for best selection; daily March-Oct 7:00-22:00, Nov-Feb 8:00-20:00, just below car park at Via del Mulini 5, tel. 089-875-489).

Vini e Panini, another small grocery, is a block from the beach a few steps above the TI. Daniela, the fifth-generation owner, speaks English and happily makes sandwiches to order. Choose from the "Caprese" (mozzarella and tomato), the "Positano" (mozzarella, tomato, and ham), or create your own (priced by weight, around €3.50-4 each). They also have a nice selection of well-priced regional wines (daily 8:00-20:00, until 22:00 in summer, closed mid-Nov-mid-March, just off church steps, tel. 089-875-175).

Positano Connections

Always check boat schedules, since the last boats often leave Positano before 18:00. The schedule varies drastically according to time of year; it's more reliable in summer than off-season, but be sure to check it with the TI. There's no real dock, so stormy weather can disrupt schedules. If you're thinking of taking a Capri trip from Positano, consider a boat that goes directly to the Blue Grotto (rather than dropping you in the port to catch another boat from there).

From Positano by Boat to: Amalfi (4-6/day, 30 minutes, €8, on TravelMar), **Capri** (mid-April-mid-Oct, 2-4/day, 30-60 minutes, €17-19; less off-season), **Sorrento** (mid-April-mid-Oct only,

2-4/day, 35 minutes, €16), **Salerno** (mid-April-Sept only, 4-6/day, 70 minutes, €12). Check schedules carefully as most boats run only mid-April to mid-October; few run off-season. Direct boats to **Naples** run several times a day in the summer (check with the TI); you can also change boats in Sorrento or Capri.

Amalfi Town

After Rome fell, the Amalfi Coast's namesake town was one of the first to trade goods—coffee, carpets, and paper—between Europe and points east. Its heyday was the 10th and 11th centuries, when it was a powerful maritime republic—a trading power with a fleet that controlled this region and rivaled Pisa, Genoa, and Venice. The Republic of Amalfi

founded a hospital in Jerusalem and claims to have founded the Knights of Malta order—even giving them the Amalfi cross, which became the famous Maltese cross. Amalfi minted its own coins and established "rules of the sea"—the basics of which survive today.

In 1343, this little powerhouse was suddenly destroyed by a tsunami caused by an undersea earthquake. That disaster, compounded by devastating plagues, left Amalfi a humble backwater. Today its 5,000 residents live off tourism. Amalfi is not as picturesque as Positano or as well-connected as Sorrento, but take some time to explore the town.

Amalfi's one main street runs up from the waterfront through a deep valley, with stairways to courtyards and houses on either side. It's worth walking uphill to the workaday upper end of town. If you hear water under a grate in the main street, it's the creek that runs through the ravine—a reminder that, originally, the town straddled the stream, and later paved over it to create a main drag. As you return downhill, be sure to explore up the winding and narrow lanes and arcaded passages on either side of the main street.

Though less touristy than Positano, Amalfi is packed during the day with big-bus tours (whose drivers pay €50 an hour to park while their groups shop for *limoncello* and ceramics). Amalfi's charms reveal themselves early and late in the day, when the tourist crowds dissipate.

Flavio Gioia

You'll see a statue of Flavio Gioia towering above the chaos of cars and buses on the seaside piazza. Amalfi residents credit this hometown boy with the invention of the magnetic compass back in 1302, but historians can't verify that he actually existed. While an improvement to the compass did occur in Amalfi during that time period, Chinese and Arab navigators had been using rudimentary compasses for years. In Gioia's time, seamen placed a magnetized needle on the surface of a container of water as a kind of medieval GPS. If Gioia existed at all, he probably just figured out how to secure that needle inside a little box. Locals, however, have no doubt that Flavio Gioia was an inventor extraordinaire.

Orientation to Amalfi Town

Amalfi's waterfront is the coast's biggest transport hub. The bus station, ferry docks, and a parking lot (€5/hour) are next to each other. A statue of local boy Flavio Gioia—the purported inventor of the compass (see sidebar)—overlooks them, and Amalfi's TI is just beyond, across the street.

Before you enter the town, notice the colorful tile above the Porta della Marina gateway, showing off the trading domain of the maritime Republic of Amalfi. Just to the left, along the busy road, is a series of arches that indicate the long, narrow, vaulted halls of its arsenal—where ships were built in the 11th century. One of these is now the fine little Arsenal Museum (described later).

Venture into the town, and you'll quickly come to Piazza Duomo, the main square, sporting a spring water-spewing statue of St. Andrew, and the cathedral—the town's most important sight.

The farther you get away from the water, the more traditional Amalfi becomes. The Paper Museum is a 10-minute walk up Via Lorenzo d'Amalfi, the main drag. From here, the road narrows and you can turn off onto a path leading to the shaded Valle dei Mulini; it's full of paper-mill ruins that recall this once proud and prosperous industry. The ruined castle clinging to the rocky ridge above Amalfi is Torre dello Ziro, a good lookout point for intrepid hikers.

Tourist Information

The TI is about 100 yards from the bus station and ferry dock, next to the post office; facing the sea, it's to the left (April-Oct Mon-Fri 9:00-13:00 & 14:00-18:00, Sat 9:00-13:00; Nov-March Mon-

Sat 9:00-13:00; closed Sun year-round; Corso della Repubbliche Marinare 27, tel. 089-871-107, www.amalfitouristoffice.it).

Helpful Hints

Don't Get Stranded: Be warned—most of the year, the last bus back to Sorrento leaves at 20:00 (at 22:00 in June-July, at 23:00 in Aug, at 21:00 in April-May and Sept—but confirm times locally) and can be full. Without a public bus, your only option is a €100 taxi ride.

Internet Access: The travel agency **L'Altra Costiera,** on the main drag a block up from the church, has Wi-Fi and computers for use (€5/hour, daily 9:00-21:00, Via Lorenzo d'Amalfi 34, tel. 089-873-6082).

Baggage Storage: You can store your bag safely for €4 at the **Divina Costiera Travel Office** facing the waterfront square, across from the bus parking area (daily 8:00-13:00 & 14:00-19:30, tel. 089-872-467).

Speedboat Charters: To hire your own boat for a tour of the coastline from Amalfi (or to Capri), consider **Charter La Dolce Vita** (mobile 335-549-9365, www.amalficoastyacht.it).

Sights in Amalfi Town

Cathedral

This church is "Amalfi Romanesque" (a mix of Moorish and Byzantine flavors, built c. 1000-1300), with a fanciful Neo-Byzantine facade from the 19th century. Climb the imposing stairway, which functions as a handy outdoor theater for town events. The 1,000-year-old bronze door at the top was given to Amalfi by a wealthy local merchant who had it made in Constantinople.

Cost and Hours: €3, daily 10:00-17:00, open only for prayer 7:30-10:00 & 17:00-19:30, tel. 089-871-324. There's a fine, free WC at the top of the steps (through unmarked green door, just a few steps before ticket booth, ask for key at desk).

Visiting the Cathedral: Pick up the English flier as you enter. Visitors are directed on a one-way circuit through the cathedral complex with four stops.

This courtyard of 120 graceful columns—the **"Cloister of Paradise"**—was the cemetery for local nobles in the 13th century (note their stone sarcophagi). Don't miss the fine view of the bell tower and its majolica tiles.

The original ninth-century church, known as the **Basilica of the Crucifix,** is now a museum filled with the art treasures of the cathedral. The Angevin Mitre (Mitra Angioina), with a "pavement of tiny pearls" setting off its gold and gems, has been worn by bishops since the 14th century. Also on display is a carved wooden decoration from a Saracen pirate ship that wrecked just outside of town in 1544 during a freak storm. Believers credit St. Andrew with causing the storm that saved the town from certain Turkish pillage and plunder.

Just as Venice needed Mark to get on the pilgrimage map, Amalfi needed St. Andrew—one of the apostles who, along with his brother (St. Peter), left their fishing nets to become the original "fishers of men." What are believed to be his remains (in the **Crypt of St. Andrew,** under the huge bronze statue) were brought here from Constantinople in 1206 during the Crusades—an indication of the wealth and importance of Amalfi back then.

The **cathedral** interior is notable for its fine 13th-century wooden crucifix. The painting behind it shows St. Andrew martyred on an X-shaped cross flanked by two Egyptian granite columns supporting a triumphal arch. Before leaving, check out the delicate mother-of-pearl crucifix (right of door in back).

▲Paper Museum

Paper has been a vital industry here since Amalfi's glory days in the Middle Ages. They'd pound rags into pulp in a big vat, pull it up using a screen, and air-dry it to create paper (the same technique used to make paper sold today in Amalfi shops). At this cavernous, cool 13th-century paper mill-turned-museum, a multilingual guide collects groups at the entrance (no particular times) for a 25-minute tour. The guide recounts the history and process of papermaking, a longtime industry for the town of Amalfi, and turns on the museum's vintage water-powered machinery. Kids can dip a screen into the rag pool and make a sheet for themselves.

Cost and Hours: €4; March-Oct daily 10:00-18:30; Nov-Feb usually Tue-Sun 10:00-15:30, closed Mon; a 10-minute walk up the main street from the cathedral, look for signs to *Museo della Carta;* tel. 089-830-4561, www.museodellacarta.it. On the way up to the museum, don't miss the huge, outdoor *presepi* (nativity scenes) on your left.

Arsenal Museum

This small, underground museum just across the road from the bus station tells the history of Amalfi's maritime glory years. Stepping into the single long room under the dramatic vaulted stone ceiling, it sinks in: A thousand years ago, they made ships here. The collection (which is well-described in English) is small, but there are plenty of historic artifacts from Amalfi's city-state days of independence (839-1135). You'll learn about the early compass "invented" here in 1302, which ultimately opened up exploration of the New World. In 1080, it was written, "This city appears opulent and popular; no other city is as rich in silver, garments, and gold. Here dwells navigators very expert at pointing out the ways of the sea and the sphere of the heavens."

Cost and Hours: €2, Tue-Sun 10:00-13:30 & 15:30-19:00, closed Mon, shorter hours off-season, Piazza Flavio Gioia, tel. 089-871-170, www.museoarsenaleamalfi.it.

Hikes

Amalfi is the starting point for several fine hikes, two of which I've described here. The TI hands out photocopies of Giovanni Visetti's trail maps (or you can download them yourself at www.giovis.com). If you can find it, the best book on hiking is Julian Tippett's *Sorrento Amalfi Capri Car Tours and Walks*. It has useful color-coded maps and info on public transportation to the trailheads.

Hike #1: Pontone

This loop trail leads up the valley past paper-mill ruins, ending in the tiny town of Pontone; you can get lunch there, and head back down to the town of Amalfi (allow 3 hours total). Bring a good map, since it's easy to veer off the main route. Start your hike by following the main road (Via Lorenzo d'Amalfi) away from the sea.

After the Paper Museum, jog right, then left to join the trail, which runs through the shaded woods along a babbling stream. Heed the signs that warn people to stay away from the ruins of paper mills (no matter how tempting), since many are ready to collapse on unwary hikers. Continue up to Pontone, where Trattoria l'Antico Borgo offers wonderful cuisine and a great view (Via Noce 4, tel. 089-871-469). After lunch, return to Amalfi via a steep stairway.

If you're feeling ambitious, before you head back to Amalfi, add a one-hour detour (30 minutes each way) to visit the ridge-hugging **Torre dello Ziro** (ask a local how to find the trail to this tower). You'll be rewarded with a spectacular view.

Hike #2: Atrani

For an easier stroll, head to the nearby town of Atrani. This village, just a 15-minute stroll beyond Amalfi town, is a world apart; its 1,500 residents consider themselves definitely *not* from Amalfi. Leave Amalfi via the main road, and stay on the water side until the sidewalk ends. Cross the street and head up the stairs; the paved route takes you over the hill, and drops you into Atrani in about 15 minutes. Piazza Umberto is the core of town, with cafés and a little grocery store that makes sandwiches. Atrani has none of the trendy resort feel of Amalfi, with relatively few tourists, a delightful town square, and a free, sandy beach (if you drive here, pay for parking at harbor). This town also has some recommended accommodations.

From Atrani, you can theoretically continue up to **Ravello**.

But be warned: Unless you're part mountain goat, you'll probably prefer catching the bus to Ravello from Amalfi town instead.

Sleeping in Amalfi Town

Sleeps are much better in Positano (nicer views) or Sorrento (lower prices), but if you're marooned in Amalfi, here are some options. Prices listed are for high season (roughly April-Oct), but can spike higher in August and drop in spring and fall.

$$ Hotel Aurora is a tranquil, bright, and cheery respite from Amalfi crowds just a 10-minute walk from the Duomo (Db-€149-189, Piazzale dei Protonini, tel. 089-871-209, www.aurora-hotel.it, info@aurora-hotel.it).

$$ Hotel Floridiana, just off the main drag and five minutes by foot from the harbor, is only three short flights of steps up from the street. Though lacking views, the 13 rooms are attractive and newly furnished and come with free garage parking—very unusual here (Db-€130-140, air-con, free Wi-Fi, Via Brancia 1; pass the Duomo, then take the next right through tiny arch—Salita Brancia—and up 30 steps; tel. 089-873-6373, www.hotelfloridiana.it, info@hotelfloridiana.it, Agnese).

$$ Hotel Lidomare's 18 rooms are decorated in traditional majolica tiles and rich antique furnishings just a few steps from the Duomo (Db-€90-145, Largo Piccolomini 9, tel. 089-871-332, www.lidomare.it, info@lidomare.it).

$ Hotel Centrale has incredible views of the cathedral in a handy, central, but noisy location (Db-€75-140, Largo Piccolomini 1, tel. 089-872-608, www.amalfihotelcentrale.it, info@amalfihotelcentrale.it).

$ Residenza del Duca is a little seven-room B&B with no views, up many flights of stairs in the heart of this touristy enclave (one minuscule Sb-€60, Db-€90—or €130 in Aug-Sept, €10 discount with this book and cash if you reserve direct, air-con, free Wi-Fi, no views but glimpses of ocean through the rooftops; 25 yards uphill from Piazza Duomo, take the first left, go up the stairs and follow the signs, then go up more stairs—over 70 total—to Via Mastalo II Duca 3; call for free luggage service—available April-Oct 8:00-20:00, tel. 089-873-6365, www.residencedelduca.it, info@residencedelduca.it, Andrea and Daniela).

Nearby, in Atrani

Atrani is a small-town hideaway without the glitz of Positano or the bustle of Amalfi. Atrani is a 15-minute hike from Amalfi (described under "Hike #2," earlier); Amalfi-Salerno buses also stop here.

$ A'Scalinatella is a dingy, informal backpackers' hostel, with a honeycomb of cramped 3- to 10-bed dorms, way-overpriced private rooms, and a communal kitchen (dorm bed-€25, D-€60, Db-€90, prices very soft—ask for Rick Steves discount on direct bookings, free Wi-Fi in common areas, 100 yards up from main square at #5 on Scalinatella Piazza Umberto I, tel. 089-871-492, www.hostelscalinatella.com, info@hostelscalinatella.com). It's run by English-speaking owners Filippo and Gabriele, who also rent rooms scattered all over town.

$ L'Argine Fiorito, which stands like a little castle overlooking a ravine at the top of town, rents five tidy and tiled rooms (Db-€105, extra bed-€35, tel. 089-873-6309, mobile 347-531-1158, www.larginefiorito.it, info@larginefiorito.it).

Eating in Amalfi Town

Amalfi, like Positano, has expensive, interchangeable restaurants along the waterfront. For a cheaper sit-down meal without a sea view, **Bar La Piazzetta** has €8-9 pasta, pizza, and salads at a dozen tables in a small, quiet square, reached through an archway directly across the main street from the cathedral steps (long hours daily, no cover, Piazza dei Dogi 5, tel. 089-871-585). Five minutes' walk up the main drag on the right (past the first archway) is **Pizza Express,** with honest €4-6 pies to go (Mon-Sat 9:00-21:00, closed Sun, Via Capuano 46, mobile 339-581-2336). The **Decò** supermarket, up an alley to the right off the main drag (by #34), is small but has a good selection (Mon-Sat 8:00-13:30 & 16:30-20:00, closed Sun, Via Dei Curiali 6).

Ravello

Ravello sits atop a lofty perch 1,000 feet above the sea. It offers an interesting church, two villas, and breathtaking views that have attracted celebrities for generations. Gore Vidal, Richard Wagner, D. H. Lawrence, M. C. Escher, Henry Wadsworth Longfellow, and Greta Garbo all have succumbed to Ravello's charms and called it home.

The town is like a lush and peaceful garden floating above it all. Wandering around, it seems there's nothing but tourists, cafés, stones, old villas-turned-luxury hotels, and grand views. It's one big place to convalesce. To me, it's more famous than enjoyable.

Ravello can make for a half-day outing

from Amalfi, or a full day from Positano with a stop in Amalfi. The views from the bus ride up and back are every bit as stunning as those along the coastal route.

To see the sights listed here, start at the bus stop and walk through the tunnel to the main square, where you'll find the Villa Rufolo on the left, the church on the right, and the **TI** down the street past the church (TI open daily May-Oct 10:00-18:00, shorter hours in winter, 100 yards from the square—follow signs to Via Roma 18, tel. 089-857-096, www.ravellotime.com). Villa Cimbrone is a 10-minute walk from the square (follow the signs).

Picnicking isn't allowed at the two villas, but there are benches with a view by the bus stop and on the main square.

Sights in Ravello

Piazza Duomo

The town's entry tunnel deposits you on the main square. Though perfectly peaceful today, the watchtower of Villa Rufolo—which used to keep an eye out for fires and invasions—is a reminder that it wasn't always postcards and *limoncello*. The facade of the cathedral is plain because the earlier, fancy west portal was destroyed in a 1364 earthquake. The front door is locked; to enter, you need to go through the museum on Viale Wagner, around the left side (described next). The fine pines on the square are pruned to look like umbrellas and provide a shady meeting place for strollers ending up here on the piazza. Opposite the church is a fine view of the terraced hillside and the community of Scala (which means "steps"—historically a way of life there). The terraces, supporting grapevines and lemon trees, mostly date from the 16th century. Viale Wagner climbs to the top of town for sea views and ruined villas that are now luxury hotels. The town is essentially traffic-free.

Duomo

Ravello's cathedral, overlooking the main square, is most memorable because its floor slopes upward. The key features of this church are its 12th-century bronze doors, with 54 Biblical scenes (from Constantinople); the carved marble pulpit supported by six lions; and the chance to climb behind the altar (left of the main altar) for a close-up look at the relic of holy blood. The geometric designs show Arabic influence. The humble cathedral museum, through which you'll enter, is two rooms of well-described carved marble that evoke the historical importance of the town.

Cost and Hours: €3 for the museum—which also gets you into the church, daily May-Oct 8:15-19:00, Nov-April 9:00-17:00, enter through the museum around the left side of the cathedral.

Villa Rufolo

The villa, built in the 13th-century ruins of a noble family's palace, presents wistful gardens among stony walls, with oh-my-God views. The Arabic/Norman gardens seem designed to frame commanding coastline vistas (you can enjoy the same view, without the entry fee, from the bus parking lot just below the villa). It's also one of the venues for Ravello's annual arts festival (July-Aug, www.ravellofestival.com) and music society performances (April-June and Sept-Oct, www.ravelloarts.org). Concertgoers perch on a bandstand on the edge of the cliff for a combination of wonderful music and dizzying views. Wagner visited here and was impressed enough to set the second act of his opera *Parsifal* in the villa's magical gardens. By all accounts, the concert on the cliff is a sublime experience.

Cost and Hours: €5, daily May-Sept 9:00-20:00, Oct-April 9:00 until sunset, may close earlier if hosting a concert, tel. 089-857-621, www.villarufolo.it.

Villa Cimbrone

This villa provides another romantic garden, this one built upon the ruins of an old convent. Located at the opposite end of Ravello, it was created in the 20th century by Englishman William Beckett. His mansion is now a five-star hotel. It's a longish walk to the end of town, where you explore a bluff dreamily landscaped around the villa. At the far end, above a sublime café on the lawn, "the Terrace of Infinity" dangles high above the sea.

Cost and Hours: €6, daily 9:00-sunset, tel. 089-858-072, www.villacimbrone.com.

▲Hike to Amalfi Town from Villa Cimbrone

To walk downhill from Ravello's Villa Cimbrone to the town of Amalfi (a path for hardy hikers only—follow the TI's map), retrace your steps back toward town. Take the first left, which turns into a stepped path winding its way below the cliff. Pause here to look back up at the rock with a big white mansion—Villa La Rondinaia, where Gore Vidal lived for many years. Continue down the fairly steep path about 40 minutes to the town of Atrani, where several bars on the main square offer well-deserved refreshment. From here, it's about a 15-minute walk back to Amalfi.

Eating in Ravello

Ristorante Da Salvatore serves a serious sit-down lunch that takes full advantage of the views that make a trip to Ravello worthwhile. Pino, the English-speaking owner of this formal restaurant, serves nicely presented, traditional Amalfi cuisine from a fun-if-pricey menu. Be adventurous when ordering and share dishes. Pato, the parakeet, is learning English (€17 pastas, €20 *secondi,* closed Mon, located at the spot where buses and taxis drop those visiting town, Via della Repubblica 2, tel. 089-857-227, reservations smart).

Ravello Connections

Ravello and the town of Amalfi are connected by a winding road and a bus. Coming from Amalfi town, buy your ticket at the bar on the waterfront, and ask where the bus stop is (normally by the statue on the waterfront, just to the statue's left as you face the water). In Ravello, line up early, since the buses are often crowded (2/hour, 25 minutes, €2.50, buy ticket in tobacco shop; catch bus 100 yards off main square, at other end of tunnel).

Paestum

The ruins at Paestum (PASTE-oom) include one of the best collections of Greek temples anywhere—and certainly the most accessible to Western Europe. Serenely situated, Paestum is surrounded by fields and wildflowers. It also has a functional zone that includes a bus stop, train station, church, and a straggle of houses and cafés that you could barely call a village.

AMALFI COAST

This town was founded as Poseidonia by Greeks in the sixth century B.C., and became a key stop on an important trade route. In the fifth century B.C., the Lucanians, a barbarous inland tribe, conquered Poseidonia and tried to adopt the cultured ways of the

Greeks. By the time of the Romans, who took over in the third century B.C., the name Poseidonia had been simplified to Paestum. The final conquerors of Paestum, malaria-carrying mosquitoes, kept the site wonderfully deserted for nearly a

thousand years. The temples were never buried—just ignored. Rediscovered in the 18th century, Paestum today offers the only well-preserved Greek ruins north of Sicily.

While most visitors do Paestum as a day trip, it's not a bad place to stay overnight. Accommodations offer great value, and though it's a bit far, you could use Paestum as a base for day-tripping to Naples or the Amalfi Coast. There's a beach nearby, and hotels can help arrange visits to local buffalo-milk dairies.

AMALFI COAST

Getting to Paestum

While Naples has direct connections to Paestum, from elsewhere you'll likely have to transfer in **Salerno** (see map).

The simplest way to reach Paestum is by **direct train from Naples' Centrale Station** (10/day, 1.5 hours, €7.50; no round-trip discount, but the €11.60 weekend-only day pass saves money, no day pass savings on weekdays). You'll need a U8 UnicoCampania regional ticket, available from *tabacchi* stores or the ticket windows at Naples' Centrale Station, which you must stamp before boarding. (Since trains to Paestum are "regional," you can't buy tickets from the automated machines at stations.) For a morning visit from Naples, you'll need to get an early start (always smart in warm weather): the first train leaves Naples at 6:30, and after the 8:30 departure, the next is at 12:52. The last three trains back from Paestum depart at 19:29, 20:45, and 21:48, arriving in Naples at 21:10, 22:26, and 23:06 (before setting off, check current times at stations or www.trenitalia.it).

From **Amalfi** or **Positano,** you can take either a bus or boat to Salerno, where you pick up the same train to Paestum on its way from Naples (35-40 minutes, €3.40). Buy your train ticket at the ticket office or the Il Globo Celeste travel agency in the Salerno train station (stamp before boarding). Buses from Amalfi terminate at the Salerno train station, but if you arrive in Salerno from the Amalfi Coast by boat, you will have to walk from the boat dock several blocks up to the train station (see the Salerno map). Alternatively, local CSTP bus #34 leaves from Piazza della Concordia in Salerno, by the base of the boat dock, for Paestum roughly every hour (1-hour trip, same €3.40 ticket). This Salerno-Paestum bus is slower than the train, and the stop is unmarked, with no posted schedule and no nearby ticket office. But it can be an option, especially during midday hours when trains are sparse. The bus brings you only slightly closer to the ruins at Paestum.

While it's technically possible to day-trip from **Sorrento** to Paestum by public transport, it makes for a very long day marred by worry about making connections back. Consider renting a car or hiring a taxi for the day. While the Amalfi Coast is a thrill to drive off-season, summer traffic is miserable. From Sorrento, Paestum is 60 miles and 3 hours via the coast, but a much smoother 2 hours by autostrada. To reach Paestum from Sorrento via the autostrada, drive toward Naples, catch the autostrada (direction: Salerno), skirt Salerno (direction: Reggio), exit at Battipaglia, and drive straight through the roundabout. During your ride, you'll see many signs for *mozzarella di bufala*, cheese made from the milk of water buffalo. Try it here—it can't be any fresher.

Planning Your Time

Allow two hours to see the ruins and the museum. Which one you see first depends on your interest and the heat. You'll enjoy the best light and smallest crowds late in the day.

Orientation to Paestum

Tourist Information: At the TI, next to the Paestum Archaeological Museum, pick up a free info booklet of the site (TI open daily 9:00-13:00 & 15:00-17:00, tel. 0828-811-016, www.infopaestum.it).

Arrival at Paestum: If you're arriving by train, exit the tiny station and walk through the old city gate; the ruins are an eight-minute walk straight ahead. (The station has no luggage storage, and its WC is usually locked.) Buses from Salerno (see "Getting to Paestum," earlier) stop near a corner of the ruins (at a little bar/café).

Cost: €10, includes site and museum.

Hours: Both museum and site are open daily at 8:30 (except the first and third Mon of each month, when the museum is closed). Year-round, the museum closes at 19:15 (last ticket sold at 18:45). The site closes one hour before sunset (as late as 19:30 June-July, as early as 15:00 in mid-Dec, last site ticket sold one hour before closing, tel. 0828-811-023).

Information: While there are scant descriptions at the site itself, this book provides all the information you need for both the site and the museum. The museum bookshop sells several mediocre guidebooks, including a €15 past-and-present guide. Dull €5 audioguides are available to rent at the museum or at site entrances (ID required). The €1.50 booklet, sold at the ticket desk, gives only general information and is more souvenir than guide.

Local Guide: Silvia Braggio is a good guide who gives a fine two-hour walk of the site and museum (special rate with this book-€100, must arrange in advance, mobile 347-643-2307, www. silviaguide.it, silvia@silviaguide.it).

Eating: La Basilica Café, between the parking lot and TI, is the most straightforward and reasonable option, with good €5-8 pizzas and other lunch fare, and free Wi-Fi (June-Sept daily 8:00-24:00, until 20:00 off-season, closed Jan, Via Magna Grecia 881, tel. 0828-811-301). **Ristorante Nettuno,** with quality food and good temple views, is more expensive and upscale (by the south entrance to the ruins).

Entry: The site and museum have separate entrances. The museum, just outside the ruins, is in a cluster with the TI and a small paleo-Christian basilica. Most visitors buy tickets at the museum and use the entrance across the street, but another ticket office and entrance is near the recommended Ristorante Nettuno (at the south end of the site). On days when the museum is closed (first and third Monday of each month), you have to buy tickets at the site entrances.

Self-Guided Tours

Paestum Archaeological Site

This tour starts at the entrance by the museum, visits the Temple of Ceres, goes through the center of the Roman town past the Greek Memorial Tomb, circles around the other two Greek temples, and then leaves the site to walk down the modern road to the Ekklesiasterion (which faces the museum).

Background: While Paestum is famous for its marvelous Greek temples, most of the structures you see are Roman. Five elements of Greek Paestum survive: three misnamed temples, a memorial tomb, and a circular meeting place (or Ekklesiasterion). The rest, including the wall that defines the site, is Roman.

Paestum was once a seaport (the ocean is now about a mile

Paestum

VIA TAVERNELLE · SP-276

CITY WALLS · IL GRANAIO DEI CASABELLA

To Agriturismo Seliano & Salerno

B To/From Salerno

TOUR BEGINS

P
LA BASILICA CAFE
ENTRANCE

TEMPLE OF CERES

100 Meters
100 Yards

EKKLESIASTERION

GREEK MEMORIAL TOMB

TICKETS

MUSEUM

TOUR ENDS

VIA MAGNA GRECIA

UNEXCAVATED AREA

SANCTUARY OF FORTUNA VIRILIS (POOL)

AMPHITHEATER

FORUM

HOTEL DELLE ROSE

To Train Station (8 minute walk)

Roman Road to Port

CURIA

VIA SACRA

Rose Garden

ANCIENT RESIDENTIAL AREA

TEMPLE OF NEPTUNE

WC

ENTRANCE (& EXIT)

TEMPLE OF HERA

STANDING RUINS

ORIGINAL FOOTPRINT

CITY WALLS

BAR/RESTAURANT NETTUNO

TICKETS

B To/From Salerno

To Sea
CITY WALLS

VIA NETTUNO

ENTRANCE

SP-189

To Hotel Villa Rita

AMALFI COAST

away—the wall in the distance, which stretches about three miles, is about halfway to today's coastline). Only about a fifth of the site has been excavated. The Greek city, which archaeologists figure had a population of about 13,000, was first conquered by Lucanians (distant relatives of the Romans, who spoke a language related to Latin), and then by the Romans (who completely made it over and built the wall you see today).

The remaining Greek structures survive because the Romans were superstitious—they respected sacred areas, and didn't mess with temples and tombs. While most old Christian churches are built upon Roman temples (it's just what people do when they conquer another culture), no Roman temple is built upon a Greek temple. Romans appreciated how religion could function as the opiate of the masses. As long as people paid their taxes and obeyed the emperor's dictates, the practical Romans had no problem with any religion. The three Greek temples that you'll see here today have stood for about 2,500 years.

• *Buy your ticket at the museum, then head to the right to find the site's north entrance. Once inside, stand in front of the...*

Temple of Ceres: All three Paestum temples have inaccurate names, coined by 19th-century archaeologists who based their

"discoveries" on wishful thinking. (While the Romans made things easy by leaving lots of inscriptions, the Greeks did not.) Those 1800s archaeologists wanted this temple to be devoted to Ceres, the goddess of agriculture. However, all the little votive statues found later, when modern archaeologists dug here, instead depicted a woman with a big helmet: Athena, goddess of wisdom and war. (The Greeks' female war goddess was also the goddess of wisdom—thinking... strategy...female. The Romans' masculine war god was Mars—just fighting.) Each temple is part of a sanctuary—an open, sacred space around the temple. Because regular people couldn't go into the temple, the altar logically stood outside.

The Temple of Ceres dates from 500 B.C. It's made of locally quarried limestone blocks. Good roads and shipping didn't come along until the Romans, so the Greeks' buildings were limited to local materials. The wooden roof is long gone. Like the other two temples, this one was once painted white, black, and red, and has an east-west orientation—facing the rising sun. This temple's *cella* (interior room) is gone, cleared out when it was used as a Christian church in the sixth century. In medieval times, Normans scavenged stones from here; chunks of these temples can be found in Amalfi's cathedral.

Walk around to the back side of the Temple of Ceres. The capitals broke in a modern earthquake, so a steel bar provides necessary support. Each of the Paestum temples is Doric style—with three stairs, columns without a base, and shafts that narrow at the top to a simple capital of a round then a square block. While there were no carved reliefs, colorful frescoes once decorated the pediments.

As you walk away, look back at the temple. Traditionally, Greeks would build a sanctuary of Athena on a city's highest spot (like the Parthenon in Athens, on the Acropolis). Paestum had no hill, so the Greeks created a mound. The hill was more impressive in its time because the Greek city level was substantially lower than the Roman pavement stones you'll walk on today.

• *From here, walk about 100 yards down the paving stones of Via Sacra toward the other Greek temples. To the left of the road, you'll see a little half-buried house with a tiled roof.*

Greek Memorial Tomb (Heroon): This tomb (from 500 b.c.) also survived because the Romans respected religious buildings. But the tomb was most inconveniently located, right in the middle of their growing city. So the practical Romans built a perimeter wall around it (visible today), added a fine tiled roof, and then buried the tomb.

There's a mystery here. Greeks generally buried their dead outside the city (as did Romans)—there are over a thousand ancient tombs outside Paestum's walls—yet this tomb was parked smack-dab in the center of town. When it was uncovered in 1952, no bodies were found inside. The tomb instead held nine perfectly preserved vases (now in the museum). Archaeologists aren't sure of the tomb's purpose. Perhaps it was a memorial dedicated to some great hero (like a city founder). Or perhaps it was a memorial to those lost when a neighboring community had to evacuate and settle as refugees here.

• *Continue walking down Via Sacra, the main drag of...*

Roman Paestum: Roman towns were garrison towns: rectangular with a grid street plan and two main streets cutting north-south and east-west, dividing the town into four equal sections. They were built by military engineers with a no-nonsense standard design. New excavations (on the left) have uncovered Roman-era lead piping. City administration buildings were on the left, and residential buildings were on the right.

Shortly after the road turns into a dirt path, you'll come to a big Roman pool that archaeologists believe was a sanctuary dedicated to Fortuna Virilis, goddess of luck and fertility. The strange stones likely supported a wooden platform for priests and statues of gods. Imagine young women walking down the ramp at the far end and through the pool, hoping to conceive a child.

The next big square was the Roman forum and ancient Paestum's main intersection. The road on the right led directly (and very practically) to the port. It made sense to have a direct connection to move freight between the sea and the center of town.

Until 2007, the vast field of ruins between the forum and the next temple (on the right) was covered in vegetation. It's since been cleared and cleaned of harmful lichen, which produce acids that dissolve limestone. Study the rocks: Yellow lichen is alive, black is dead. Even the great temples of Paestum were covered in this destructive lichen until 2000, when a two-year-long project cleaned them for the first time.

• *Ahead on the left are the so-called...*

Temples of Neptune and Hera: The **Temple of Neptune** dates from 450 B.C. and employs the Greek architectural trick where the

base line is curved up just a tad, to overcome the illusion of sagging caused by a straight base. The Athenians built their Parthenon (with a similar bowed-up base line) just 30 years after this. Many think this temple could have been their inspiration.

The adjacent **Temple of Hera,** dating from 550 B.C., is the oldest of Paestum's three temples and one of the oldest Greek temples still standing anywhere.

Notice the change 100 years makes in the architectural styles: Archaic Doric in 550 B.C. versus Classic Doric in 450 B.C.

Archaeologists now believe the "Temple of Neptune" was actually devoted to a different god. Votive statues uncovered here suggest that Hera was the focus (perhaps this was a new and improved version of the adjacent, simpler, and older Temple of Hera). Or perhaps it was a temple to Zeus, Hera's husband, to honor the couple together.

Together, the two temples formed a single huge sanctuary with altars on the far (east) side. Walk around to the front. Notice how overbuilt the Temple of Hera appears. Its columns and capitals are closer together than necessary, as if the builders lacked confidence in their ability to span the distance between supports. Square pillars mark the corners of the *cella* inside. Temples with an odd number of columns (here, nine) had a single colonnade crossing in the center inside to support the wooden roof. More modern temples (such as the Temple of Neptune) had six columns, with two colonnades passing through the *cella*. This left a line of vision open through the middle so that worshippers could see the big statue of the god.

By the way, in 1943, Allied paratroopers dropped in near here during the famous "Landing of Salerno," when the Allies (who had already taken Sicily) invaded mainland Italy. Paestum was part of their first beachhead. The Temple of Hera served as an Allied military tent hospital. From here, the Allies pushed back the Nazis, marching to Naples, Cassino, and finally to Rome.

• *Leave the site and turn left on the modern road, Via Magna Grecia. The king of Naples had this Naples-to-Paestum road built in 1829 to inspire his people with ancient temples. While he was modern in his appreciation of antiquity, his road project destroyed a swath of the ancient city, as you'll see as you pass by half of the small amphitheater. Just past the amphitheater, you'll find the...*

Ekklesiasterion: Immediately across the street from the museum is what looks like a sunken circular theater. This rare bit of ancient Greek ruins was the Ekklesiasterion, a meeting place where the Greeks would get together to discuss things and vote. Archaeologists believe that the agora (market) would also have been located here.

• *Across the street is the...*

Paestum Archaeological Museum

Paestum's museum offers the rare opportunity to see artifacts—dating from prehistoric to Greek to Roman times—at the site where they were discovered. These beautifully crafted works (with good English descriptions throughout) help bring Paestum to life. Not everything you see here is from Paestum, though, as the museum also collects artifacts from other nearby sites.

Before stepping into the museum, notice the proud fascist architecture. Though the building dates from 1954, it was designed in 1938. It seems to command that you *will* enjoy this history lesson.

The exhibit is on several levels. You'll find mostly Greek pieces on the ground floor (artifacts from the Temple of Hera in front, frescoes from tombs in the back), Paleolithic to Iron Age artifacts on the mezzanine level, and Roman art on the top floor (statues, busts, and inscriptions dating from the time of the Roman occupation). While Roman art is not unique to Paestum, the Greek collection is—so that's what you should focus on. Here are the highlights:

Temple Reliefs: The museum's first room is designed like a Greek temple, with an inner *cella* that is used for temporary exhibitions. The large carvings overhead that wrap around this inner sanctum once adorned a sanctuary of the goddess Hera (wife of Zeus) five miles away. This sanctuary, called Heraion del Sele, was discovered and excavated in 1934. Some of the carvings show

AMALFI COAST

scenes from the life of Hercules. To the left side, displays tell the story of the excavation of both Heraion del Sele and Paestum.

• *Along the back wall of this room, find the glass case holding nine perfectly preserved...*

Vases: One ceramic and eight bronze, with artistic handles, these vases were found in Paestum's Greek Memorial Tomb (described earlier). Greek bronzes are rare because Romans often melted them down to make armor. These were discovered in 1952, filled with still-liquid honey and sealed with beeswax. The honey (as you can see in the display cases below) has since crystallized. Honey was a standard part of a funeral because, to ancient Greeks, honey symbolized immortality...it lasts forever.

• *The next room is filled with ancient Greek...*

Votive Offerings: These were dug up at Heraion del Sele (not at Paestum). Such offerings are a huge help to modern archaeologists, since the figures worshippers brought to a temple are clues as to which god the temple honored. These votives depict a woman with a crown on a throne—clearly Hera. The clay votives were simple, affordable, and accessible to regular people.

• *Now enter the large room (broken up by pillars and interior walls) that holds...*

Relics from the Temples at Paestum: This room displays smaller pieces that have been dug up at the site. Paestum's three temples were once adorned with decorations, such as ornamental spouts that spurted rainwater out of lions' mouths. Notice the bits of the surviving black, red, and white paint, and the reconstructions showing archaeologists' best guesses as to how the original decorations might have looked.

Displays (mostly in Italian) tell in which temple each relic was found. The Temple of Ceres is often referred to as the Temple of Athena or as the northern (*settentrionale)* sanctuary. The Temples of Neptune and Hera are spoken of as the southern (*meridionale*) sanctuaries. A fine drawing by Piranesi is on display, showing his visit to Paestum in 1777.

• *In a glass case nearby, find the statue of...*

Zeus: This painted clay statue of Zeus dates from 520 B.C. The king of the gods was so lusty with his antics, he's still smirking.

• *Look out the museum's back window for a good...*

View of Paestum's Walls: The walls of ancient Paestum reach halfway to the mountain—a reminder that most of the site is still private property and yet to be excavated. The town up on the mountainside is Capaccio, established in the eighth century when inhabitants of the original city of Paestum were driven out by malaria and the city was abandoned.

• *Walk along the corridor at the back of the museum, which shows...*

Objects from Tombs: Over 1,000 tombs have been identified outside of the ancient city's wall. About 100 were found decorated with frescoes or containing objects such as these.

• *At the far end of the corridor, turn left to see...*

The Tomb of the Diver: This is the museum's treasure and the most precious Paestum find. Dating from 480 B.C., it's not only the

sole ancient Greek tomb fresco in the museum—it's the only one ever found in southern Italy. Discovered in 1968, it has five frescoed slabs (four sides and a lid; the bottom wasn't decorated). The Greeks saw death as a passage: diving from mortality into immortality...into an un-

known world. Archaeologists believe that the pillars shown on the fresco represent the Pillars of Hercules at Gibraltar, which in ancient times defined the known world. The ocean beyond the Mediterranean was the great unknown...like the afterlife. The Greek banquet makes it clear that this was an aristocratic man.

• *After the Tomb of the Diver, the next room displays...*

Lucanian Tomb Frescoes: The many other painted slabs in the museum date from a later time, around 350 B.C., when Paestum fell under Lucanian rule. These frescoes are cruder than their earlier Greek counterpart. The people who conquered the Greeks tried to appropriate their art and style, but they lacked the Greeks' distinctive light touch. Still, these offer fascinating glimpses into ancient life here at Paestum.

• *Beyond this room, you'll find yourself back at the entrance. Before you leave, go up the stairs by the bookshop for a glimpse at the mezzanine level, which focuses on prehistoric archaeology. The exhibit here has much better English translations than the ground floor. At the very least, check out the...*

Film Footage from WWII: A 10-minute continuous film loop, subtitled in English, tells the story of Allied soldiers' encounters with the ruins in 1943. You'll see footage of soldiers hanging up their laundry and shaving in the temples, which they actually safeguarded well. Part of the film focuses on excavations directed by a British archaeologist who was attached to the invading forces.

Sleeping in Paestum

Paestum at night, with views of the floodlit ruins, is magic. Accommodations here offer great value. You can sleep in a mansion for the same price you'd pay for a closet in Positano. The prices listed are for high season (which rise further in August). All have free parking.

$ Il Granaio dei Casabella, a converted old granary with 14 attractive, reasonably priced rooms, is a 10-minute walk from the ruins. It has a beautiful garden and pretty common areas, and four rooms have views of one of the ancient temples (Sb-€70, Db-€90, Tb-€110, Qb-€130, about €20 more per room mid-July-Aug, 10 percent discount for Rick Steves readers, air-con, free Wi-Fi, just west of the bus stop closest to Salerno at Via Tavernelle 84, tel. 0828-721-014, www.ilgranaiodeicasabella.com, info@ilgranaio-deicasabella.com, hospitable Celardo family).

$ Hotel Villa Rita is a tidy, quiet country hotel set on two acres within walking distance of the beach and the temples. It has 22 rooms, a kid-friendly swimming pool, and attractive grounds with grassy lawns and a little soccer field (Sb-€70, Db-€90-100, €130 in Aug, third bed-€15, lunch or dinner-€16, Luigi promises a 10 percent discount with this book and cash in 2014, air-con, free Wi-Fi, closed Nov-Feb, Via Nettuno 9, tel. 0828-811-081, www.hotelvillarita.it, info@hotelvillarita.it). The hotel is a 10-minute walk west of the Hera entrance and public bus stop, and a 20-minute walk from the train station (they can usually pick you up, if you're arriving with luggage).

$ Hotel delle Rose, with 10 small, basic rooms with minuscule bathrooms, is near the Neptune entrance on the street bordering the ruins. It's an acceptable choice for those on a budget and is also the option closest to the ruins and the train station (Sb-€35, Db-€60, Tb-€70, Qb-€85, Luigi promises these prices in 2014 if you mention this book and reserve direct, Via Magna Grecia 943, tel. 0828-199-0692, www.hotelristorantedellerose.com, info@hotelristorantedellerose.com).

Nearby

$ Agriturismo Seliano is a great option for drivers only. It offers plush public spaces, a pool, and 14 grand, spacious rooms on a peaceful, once-elegant farm estate that's been in the same family for 300 years (Db-€80-90, €110 in Aug, air-con, guest computer, free Wi-Fi, closed Nov-March; one mile north of ruins on main road—Via Magna Grecia—a small *Azienda Agrituristica Seliano* sign directs you down long dirt driveway; Via Seliano, tel. 0828-723-634, www.agriturismoseliano.it, seliano@agriturismoseliano.it). They serve a fine lunch or dinner with produce fresh from the garden (€20 for guests or €25 for non-guests, price includes all your drinks). The place is run by Cecilia, an English-speaking baroness, and her family—including about a dozen dogs.

Paestum Connections

By Train: Ten slow, milk-run trains a day head to Salerno (40 minutes, €3.40) and Naples (1.5 hours, €7.50). In Salerno, you can change for the bus to Amalfi, or walk down to the harbor to catch an Amalfi- or Positano-bound boat. Buy your train ticket at the bar-café near the Paestum TI or various souvenir shops—the station is not staffed. The last train out is at 21:48 (recheck times at station).

By Bus to Salerno: Buses from Paestum to Salerno run roughly every hour (1 hour, last departure about 20:00, €3.40). Buy a ticket from one of the bars in Paestum, then go to either of the intersections that flank the ruins, flag down any northbound bus, and ask, "Salerno?" From Salerno, you can continue on to Amalfi or Positano by boat, or walk up to the train station to catch an Amalfi-bound SITA bus or a train. Salerno's **TI** has bus, ferry, and train schedules (Mon-Sat 9:00-13:00 & 15:15-19:15, closed Sun, shorter hours off-season, on Piazza Veneto, just outside train station, tel. 089-231-432, toll-free 800-213-289, www.turismoinsalerno.it).

AMALFI COAST

PRACTICALITIES

This section covers just the basics on traveling in Italy (for much more information, see *Rick Steves' Italy*). You can find free advice on specific topics at www.ricksteves.com/tips.

Money

Italy uses the euro currency: 1 euro (€) = about $1.30. To convert prices in euros to dollars, add about 30 percent: €20 = about $26, €50 = about $65. (Check www.oanda.com for the latest exchange rates.)

The standard way for travelers to get euros is to withdraw money from ATMs (which locals call a *bancomat*) using a debit or credit card, ideally with a Visa or MasterCard logo. Before departing, call your bank or credit-card company: Confirm that your card will work overseas, ask about international transaction fees, and alert them that you'll be making withdrawals in Europe. Also ask for the PIN number for your credit card in case it'll help you use Europe's "chip-and-PIN" payment machines (see below); allow time for your bank to mail your PIN to you. To keep your valuables safe while traveling, wear a money belt.

Dealing with "Chip and PIN": Much of Europe (including Italy) is adopting a "chip-and-PIN" system for credit cards, and some merchants rely on it exclusively. European chip-and-PIN cards are embedded with an electronic chip, in addition to the magnetic stripe used on our American-style cards. This means that your credit (and debit) card might not work at automated payment machines, such as those at train and subway stations, toll roads, parking garages, luggage lockers, and self-serve gas pumps. Memorizing your credit card's PIN lets you use it at some chip-and-PIN machines—just enter your PIN when prompted. If a payment machine won't take your card, look for a machine that takes cash or see if there's a cashier nearby who can process your transaction. The easiest solution is to pay for your purchases with cash you've withdrawn from an ATM using your debit card (Europe's ATMs still accept magnetic-stripe cards).

Phoning

Smart travelers use the telephone to reserve or reconfirm rooms, reserve restaurants, get directions, research transportation connections, confirm tour times, phone home, and lots more.

To call Italy from the US or Canada: Dial 011-39 and then the local number. (The 011 is our international access code, and 39 is Italy's country code.)

To call Italy from a European country: Dial 00-39 followed by the local number. (The 00 is Europe's international access code.)

To call within Italy: Just dial the local number.

To call from Italy to another country: Dial 00 followed by the country code (for example, 1 for the US or Canada), then the area code and number. If you're calling European countries whose phone numbers begin with 0, you'll usually have to omit that 0 when you dial.

Tips on Phoning: A mobile phone—whether an American one that works in Italy, or a European one you buy when you arrive—is handy, but can be pricey. If traveling with a smartphone, switch off data-roaming until you have free Wi-Fi. If you have a smartphone, you can use it to make free or inexpensive calls in Europe by using a calling app such as Skype or FaceTime when you're on Wi-Fi.

To make cheap international calls from any phone (even your hotel-room phone), you can buy an international phone card in Italy. These work with a scratch-to-reveal PIN code, allow you to call home to the US for pennies a minute, and also work for domestic calls.

Another option is buying an insertable phone card in Italy. These are usable only at pay phones, are reasonable for making calls within the country, and work for international calls as well (though not as cheaply as the international phone cards). Note that insertable phone cards—and most international phone cards—work only in the country where you buy them.

Calling from your hotel-room phone is usually expensive, unless you use an international phone card. For more on phoning, see www.ricksteves.com/phoning.

Making Hotel Reservations

To ensure the best value, I recommend reserving rooms in advance, particularly during peak season. Email the hotelier with the following key pieces of information: number and type of rooms;

From:	rick@ricksteves.com
Sent:	Today
To:	info@hotelcentral.com
Subject:	Reservation request for 19-22 July

Dear Hotel Central,

I would like to reserve a double room for 2 people for 3 nights, arriving 19 July and departing 22 July. If possible, I would like a quiet room with a bathroom inside the room.

Please let me know if you have a room available and the price.

Thank you!
Rick Steves

number of nights; date of arrival; date of departure; and any special requests. (For a sample form, see sidebar above.) Use the European style for writing dates: day/month/year. For example, for a two-night stay in July, you could request: "1 double room for 2 nights, arrive 16/07/14, depart 18/07/14." Hoteliers typically ask for your credit-card number as a deposit.

Given the economic downturn, hoteliers are often willing and eager to make a deal—try emailing several to ask their best price. In general, hotel prices can soften if you do any of the following: offer to pay cash, stay at least three nights, or mention this book. You can also try asking for a cheaper room or a discount, or offer to skip breakfast.

Eating

Italy offers a wide array of eateries. A *ristorante* is a formal restaurant, while a *trattoria* or *osteria* is usually more traditional and simpler (but can still be pricey). Italian "bars" are not taverns, but small cafés selling sandwiches, coffee, and other drinks. An *enoteca* is a wine bar with snacks and light meals. Take-away food from pizza shops and delis (such as a *rosticceria* or *tavola calda*) makes an easy picnic.

Italians eat dinner a bit later than we do; better restaurants start serving around 19:00. A full meal consists of an appetizer (antipasto), a first course (*primo piatto*, pasta, rice, or soup), and a second course (*secondo piatto*, expensive meat and fish/seafood dishes). Vegetables *(verdure)* may come with the *secondo*, but more often must be ordered separately as a side dish (*contorno*). Desserts (*dolci*) can be very tempting. The euros can add up in a hurry, but you don't have to order each course. My approach is to mix antipasti and *primi piatti* family-style with my dinner partners (skipping *secondi*). Or, for a basic value, look for a *menù del giorno*, a three- or four-course, fixed-price meal deal (avoid the cheapest ones, often called a *menù turistico*).

Good service is relaxed (slow to an American). You won't get the bill until you ask for it: *"Il conto?"* Most restaurants include a service charge in their prices (check the menu for *servizio incluso*—generally around 15 percent). To reward good service, add a euro or two for each person in your party. If you order at a counter rather than from waitstaff, there's no need to tip. Many (but not all) restaurants in Italy add a cover charge *(coperto)* of €1-3.50 per person to your bill.

At bars and cafés, getting a drink while standing at the bar *(banco)* is cheaper than drinking it at a table *(tavolo)* or sitting outside *(terrazza)*. This tiered pricing system is clearly posted on the wall. Sometimes you'll pay at a cash register, then take the receipt to another counter to claim your drink.

Transportation

By Train: In Italy, most travelers find it's cheapest simply to buy train tickets as they go. To see if a railpass could save you money, check www.ricksteves.com/rail. To research train schedules, visit Germany's excellent all-Europe website, www.bahn.com, or Italy's www.trenitalia.com. A private company called Italo is also running fast trains on major routes in Italy; see www.italotreno.it.

You can buy tickets at train stations (at the ticket window or at automated machines with English instructions) or from travel agencies. Before boarding the train, you must validate your train documents by stamping them in the machine near the platform (usually marked *convalida biglietti* or *vidimazione*). Strikes *(sciopero)* are common and generally announced in advance (but a few sporadic trains still run—ask around).

By Car: It's cheaper to arrange most car rentals from the US. For tips on your insurance options, see www.ricksteves.com/cdw, and for route planning, consult www.viamichelin.com. Theft insurance is mandatory in Italy ($15-20/day). Bring your driver's license. You're also technically required to have an International Driving Permit (sold at your local AAA office for $15 plus the cost of two passport-type photos; see www.aaa.com).

Italy's freeway *(autostrada)* system is slick and speedy, but you'll pay about a dollar for every 10 minutes of use. Be warned that car traffic is restricted in many city centers—don't drive or park in any area that has a sign reading *Zona Traffico Limitato* (*ZTL*, often shown above a red circle)...or you might be mailed a ticket later.

Local road etiquette is similar to that in the US. Ask your car-rental company about the rules of the road, or check the US State Department website (www.travel.state.gov, click on "International Travel," then specify your country of choice and click "Traffic Safety and Road Conditions").

PRACTICALITIES

A car is a worthless headache in cities—park it safely (get tips from your hotel). As break-ins are common, be sure all of your valuables are out of sight and locked in the trunk, or even better, with you or in your hotel room.

Helpful Hints

Emergency Help: For English-speaking **police** help, dial 113. To summon an **ambulance**, call 118. For passport problems, call the **US Embassy** (in Rome, 24-hour line—tel. 06-46741) or **US Consulates** (Milan—tel. 02-290-351, Florence—tel. 055-266-951, Naples—tel. 081-583-8111); or the **Canadian Embassy** (in Rome, tel. 06-854-441). For other concerns, get advice from your hotelier.

Theft or Loss: Italy has particularly hardworking pickpockets—wear a money belt. Assume beggars are pickpockets and any scuffle is simply a distraction by a team of thieves. If you stop for any commotion or show, put your hands in your pockets before someone else does.

To replace a passport, you'll need to go in person to an embassy or consulate (see above). Cancel and replace your credit and debit cards by calling these 24-hour US numbers collect: Visa—tel. 303/967-1096, MasterCard—tel. 636/722-7111, American Express—tel. 336/393-1111. File a police report either on the spot or within a day or two; you'll need it to submit an insurance claim for lost or stolen railpasses or travel gear, and it can help with replacing your passport or credit and debit cards. Precautionary measures can minimize the effects of loss—back up your digital photos and other files frequently. For more information, see www.ricksteves.com/help.

Time: Italy uses the 24-hour clock. It's the same through 12:00 noon, then keep going: 13:00, 14:00, and so on. Italy, like most of continental Europe, is six/nine hours ahead of the East/West Coasts of the US.

Business Hours: Many businesses have now adopted the government's recommended 8:00 to 14:00 workday (although in tourist areas, shops are open longer). Still, expect small towns and villages to be more or less shut tight during the midafternoon. Stores are also usually closed on Sunday, and often on Monday.

Sights: Opening and closing hours of sights can change unexpectedly; confirm the latest times with the local tourist information office or its website. Some major churches enforce a modest dress code (no bare shoulders or shorts) for everyone, even children.

Holidays and Festivals: Italy celebrates many holidays, which can close sights and attract crowds (book hotel rooms ahead). For information on holidays and festivals, check Italy's website: www.italia.it. For a simple list showing major—though not all—events, see www.ricksteves.com/festivals.

PRACTICALITIES

Numbers and Stumblers: What Americans call the second floor of a building is the first floor in Europe. Europeans write dates as day/month/year, so Christmas is 25/12/14. Commas are decimal points and vice versa—a dollar and a half is 1,50, and there are 5.280 feet in a mile. Italy uses the metric system: A kilogram is 2.2 pounds; a liter is about a quart; and a kilometer is six-tenths of a mile.

Resources from Rick Steves

This Snapshot guide is excerpted from my latest edition of *Rick Steves' Italy,* which is one of more than 30 titles in my series of guidebooks on European travel. I also produce a public television series, *Rick Steves' Europe,* and a public radio show, *Travel with Rick Steves.* My website, www.ricksteves.com, offers free travel information, a Graffiti Wall for travelers' comments, guidebook updates, my travel blog, an online travel store, and information on European railpasses and our tours of Europe. If you're bringing a mobile device on your trip, you can download free information from Rick Steves Audio Europe, featuring podcasts of my radio shows, free audio tours of major sights in Europe, and travel interviews about Italy (via www.ricksteves.com/audioeurope, iTunes, Google Play, or the Rick Steves Audio Europe free smartphone app). You can follow me on Facebook and Twitter.

Additional Resources

Tourist Information: www.italia.it
Passports and Red Tape: www.travel.state.gov
Travel Insurance Tips: www.ricksteves.com/insurance
Packing List: www.ricksteves.com/packlist
Cheap Flights: www.kayak.com
Airplane Carry-on Restrictions: www.tsa.gov/travelers
Updates for This Book: www.ricksteves.com/update

How Was Your Trip?

If you'd like to share your tips, concerns, and discoveries after using this book, please fill out the survey at www.ricksteves.com/feedback. Thanks in advance—it helps a lot.

Italian Survival Phrases

English	Italian	Pronunciation
Good day.	*Buon giorno.*	bwohn **jor**-noh
Do you speak English?	*Parla inglese?*	**par**-lah een-**glay**-zay
Yes. / No.	*Sì. / No.*	see / noh
I (don't) understand.	*(Non) capisco.*	(nohn) kah-**pees**-koh
Please.	*Per favore.*	pehr fah-**voh**-ray
Thank you.	*Grazie.*	**graht**-seeay
You're welcome.	*Prego.*	**pray**-go
I'm sorry.	*Mi dispiace.*	mee dee-speeah-chay
Excuse me.	*Mi scusi.*	mee **skoo**-zee
(No) problem.	*(Non) c'è un problema.*	(nohn) cheh oon proh-**blay**-mah
Good.	*Va bene.*	vah **behn**-ay
Goodbye.	*Arrivederci.*	ah-ree-vay-**dehr**-chee
one / two	*uno / due*	**oo**-noh / **doo**-ay
three / four	*tre / quattro*	tray / **kwah**-troh
five / six	*cinque / sei*	**cheeng**-kway / **seh**ee
seven / eight	*sette / otto*	**seht**-tay / **ot**-toh
nine / ten	*nove / dieci*	**nov**-ay / dee**eay**-chee
How much is it?	*Quanto costa?*	**kwahn**-toh **kos**-tah
Write it?	*Me lo scrive?*	may loh **skree**-vay
Is it free?	*È gratis?*	eh **grah**-tees
Is it included?	*È incluso?*	eh een-**kloo**-zoh
Where can I buy / find...?	*Dove posso comprare / trovare...?*	**doh**-vay **pos**-soh kohm-**prah**-ray / troh-**vah**-ray
I'd like / We'd like...	*Vorrei / Vorremmo...*	vor-**reh**ee / vor-**ray**-moh
...a room.	*...una camera.*	**oo**-nah **kah**-meh-rah
...a ticket to ____.	*...un biglietto per ____.*	oon beel-**yeht**-toh pehr
Is it possible?	*È possibile?*	eh poh-**see**-bee-lay
Where is...?	*Dov'è...?*	**doh**-veh
...the train station	*...la stazione*	lah staht-seeoh-nay
...the bus station	*...la stazione degli autobus*	lah staht-seeoh-nay **dayl**-yee **ow**-toh-boos
...tourist information	*...informazioni per turisti*	een-for-maht-seeoh-nee pehr too-**ree**-stee
...the toilet	*...la toilette*	lah twah-**leht**-tay
men	*uomini, signori*	**woh**-mee-nee, seen-**yoh**-ree
women	*donne, signore*	**don**-nay, seen-**yoh**-ray
left / right	*sinistra / destra*	see-**nee**-strah / **dehs**-trah
straight	*sempre diritto*	**sehm**-pray dee-**ree**-toh
When do you open / close?	*A che ora aprite / chiudete?*	ah kay **oh**-rah ah-**pree**-tay / keeoo-**day**-tay
At what time?	*A che ora?*	ah kay **oh**-rah
Just a moment.	*Un momento.*	oon moh-**mayn**-toh
now / soon / later	*adesso / presto / tardi*	ah-**dehs**-soh / **prehs**-toh / **tar**-dee
today / tomorrow	*oggi / domani*	**oh**-jee / doh-**mah**-nee

In an Italian-speaking Restaurant

English	Italian	Pronunciation
I'd like...	Vorrei...	vor-**rehee**
We'd like...	Vorremmo...	vor-**ray**-moh
...to reserve...	...prenotare...	pray-noh-**tah**-ray
...a table for one / two.	...un tavolo per uno / due.	oon **tah**-voh-loh pehr **oo**-noh / **doo**-ay
Non-smoking.	Non fumare.	nohn foo-**mah**-ray
Is this seat free?	È libero questo posto?	eh **lee**-bay-roh **kwehs**-toh **poh**-stoh
The menu (in English), please.	Il menù (in inglese), per favore.	eel may-**noo** (een een-**glay**-zay) pehr fah-**voh**-ray
service (not) included	servizio (non) incluso	sehr-**veet**-seeoh (nohn) een-**kloo**-zoh
cover charge	pane e coperto	**pah**-nay ay koh-**pehr**-toh
to go	da portar via	dah **por**-tar **vee**-ah
with / without	con / senza	kohn / **sehn**-sah
and / or	e / o	ay / oh
menu (of the day)	menù (del giorno)	may-**noo** (dayl **jor**-noh)
specialty of the house	specialità della casa	spay-chah-lee-**tah dehl**-lah **kah**-zah
first course (pasta, soup)	primo piatto	**pree**-moh peeah-toh
main course (meat, fish)	secondo piatto	say-**kohn**-doh peeah-toh
side dishes	contorni	kohn-**tor**-nee
bread	pane	**pah**-nay
cheese	formaggio	for-**mah**-joh
sandwich	panino	pah-**nee**-noh
soup	minestra, zuppa	mee-**nehs**-trah, **tsoo**-pah
salad	insalata	een-sah-**lah**-tah
meat	carne	**kar**-nay
chicken	pollo	**poh**-loh
fish	pesce	**peh**-shay
seafood	frutti di mare	**froo**-tee dee **mah**-ray
fruit / vegetables	frutta / legumi	**froo**-tah / lay-**goo**-mee
dessert	dolci	**dohl**-chee
tap water	acqua del rubinetto	**ah**-kwah dayl roo-bee-**nay**-toh
mineral water	acqua minerale	**ah**-kwah mee-nay-**rah**-lay
milk	latte	**lah**-tay
(orange) juice	succo (d'arancia)	**soo**-koh (dah-**rahn**-chah)
coffee / tea	caffè / tè	kah-**feh** / teh
wine	vino	**vee**-noh
red / white	rosso / bianco	**roh**-soh / bee**ahn**-koh
glass / bottle	bicchiere / bottiglia	bee-kee**ay**-ray / boh-**teel**-yah
beer	birra	**bee**-rah
Cheers!	Cin cin!	cheen cheen
More. / Another.	Ancora un po.' / Un altro.	ahn-**koh**-rah oon poh / oon **ahl**-troh
The same.	Lo stesso.	loh **stehs**-soh
The bill, please.	Il conto, per favore.	eel **kohn**-toh pehr fah-**voh**-ray
tip	mancia	**mahn**-chah
Delicious!	Delizioso!	day-leet-seeoh-zoh

For more user-friendly Italian phrases, check out *Rick Steves' Italian Phrase Book & Dictionary* or *Rick Steves' French, Italian, and German Phrase Book.*

INDEX

INDEX

Audio Europe™

Rick's Free Travel App

Get your FREE **Rick Steves Audio Europe**™ app to enjoy…

- Dozens of self-guided tours of Europe's top museums, sights and historic walks

- Hundreds of tracks filled with cultural insights and sightseeing tips from Rick's radio interviews

- All organized into handy geographic playlists

- For iPhone, iPad, iPod Touch, Android

With Rick whispering in your ear, Europe gets even better.

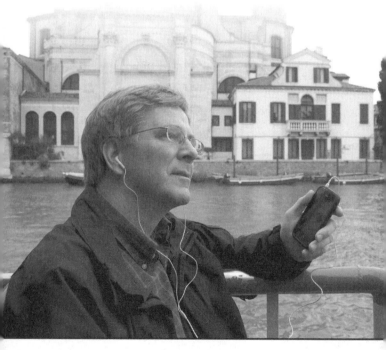

Find out more at ricksteves.com

Join
a Rick
Steves
tour

**Enjoy Europe's
warmest welcome...
with the flexibility and
friendship of a small group
getting to know Rick's
favorite places and people.
It all starts with our free
tour catalog and DVD.**

**Great guides, small
groups, no grumps.**

See more than three dozen itineraries throughout Europe

▶ Explore Europe

Browse thousands of articles, video clips, photos and radio interviews, plus find a wealth of money-saving tips for planning your dream trip. You'll find up-to-date information on Europe's best destinations, packing smart, getting around, finding rooms, staying healthy, avoiding scams and more.

▶ Travel News

Subscribe to our free Travel News e-newsletter, and get monthly updates from Rick on what's happening in Europe!

▶ Travel Forums

Learn, ask, share—our online community of savvy travelers is a great resource for first-time travelers to Europe, as well as seasoned pros.

▶ Rick's Free Audio Europe™ App

The Rick Steves Audio Europe™ app brings history and art to life. Enjoy Rick's audio tours of Europe's top museums, sights and neighborhood walks—plus hundreds of tracks including travel tips and cultural insights from Rick's radio show—all organized into geographic playlists. Learn more at ricksteves.com.

▶ Great Gear from Rick's Travel Store

Pack light and right—on a budget—with Rick's custom-designed carry-on bags, wheeled bags, day packs, travel accessories, guidebooks, journals, maps and Blu-ray/DVDs of his TV shows.

130 Fourth Avenue North, PO Box 2009 • Edmonds, WA 98020 USA
Phone: (425) 771-8303 • Fax: (425) 771-0833 • ricksteves.com

www.ricksteves.com

EUROPE GUIDES

Best of Europe
Eastern Europe
Europe Through the Back Door
Mediterranean Cruise Ports
Northern European Cruise Ports

COUNTRY GUIDES

Croatia & Slovenia
England
France
Germany
Great Britain
Ireland
Italy
Portugal
Scandinavia
Spain
Switzerland

CITY & REGIONAL GUIDES

Amsterdam, Bruges & Brussels
Barcelona
Budapest
Florence & Tuscany
Greece: Athens & the Peloponnese
Istanbul
London
Paris
Prague & the Czech Republic
Provence & the French Riviera
Rome
Venice
Vienna, Salzburg & Tirol

SNAPSHOT GUIDES

Berlin
Bruges & Brussels
Copenhagen & the Best of
   Denmark
Dublin
Dubrovnik
Hill Towns of Central Italy
Italy's Cinque Terre
Krakow, Warsaw & Gdansk
Lisbon
Madrid & Toledo
Milan & the Italian Lakes District
Munich, Bavaria & Salzburg
Naples & the Amalfi Coast
Northern Ireland
Norway
Scotland
Sevilla, Granada & Southern Spain
Stockholm

POCKET GUIDES

Amsterdam
Athens
Barcelona
Florence
London
Paris
Rome
Venice

Rick Steves guidebooks are published by Avalon Travel,
a member of the Perseus Books Group.

NOW AVAILABLE:
eBOOKS, DVD & BLU-RAY

TRAVEL CULTURE

Europe 101
European Christmas
Postcards from Europe
Travel as a Political Act

eBOOKS

Nearly all Rick Steves guides are available as eBooks. Check with your favorite bookseller.

RICK STEVES' EUROPE DVDs

11 New Shows 2013–2014
Austria & the Alps
Eastern Europe
England & Wales
European Christmas
European Travel Skills & Specials
France
Germany, BeNeLux & More
Greece, Turkey & Portugal
Iran
Ireland & Scotland
Italy's Cities
Italy's Countryside
Scandinavia
Spain
Travel Extras

BLU-RAY

Celtic Charms
Eastern Europe Favorites
European Christmas
Italy Through the Back Door
Mediterranean Mosaic
Surprising Cities of Europe

PHRASE BOOKS & DICTIONARIES

French
French, Italian & German
German
Italian
Portuguese
Spanish

JOURNALS

Rick Steves' Pocket Travel Journal
Rick Steves' Travel Journal

PLANNING MAPS

Britain, Ireland & London
Europe
France & Paris
Germany, Austria & Switzerland
Ireland
Italy
Spain & Portugal

Rick Steves books and DVDs are available at bookstores and through online booksellers.

Avalon Travel
a member of the Perseus Books Group
1700 Fourth Street
Berkeley, CA 94710

Text © 2013. All rights reserved.
Maps © 2013 by Europe Through the Back Door. All rights reserved.
Portions of this book originally appeared in *Rick Steves' Italy 2014.*

Photos are used by permission and are the property of the original copyright owners.

Printed in Canada by Friesens
Second printing June 2014

ISBN 978-1-61238-684-3

For the latest on Rick's lectures, guidebooks, tours, public radio show, and public television series, contact Europe Through the Back Door, Box 2009, Edmonds, WA 98020, tel. 425/771-8303, fax 425/771-0833, www.ricksteves.com, rick@ricksteves.com.

Europe Through the Back Door

Managing Editor: Risa Laib
Editorial & Production Manager: Jennifer Madison Davis
Editors: Glenn Eriksen, Tom Griffin, Cameron Hewitt, Suzanne Kotz, Cathy Lu, Carrie Shepherd, Gretchen Strauch
Editorial Assistant: Jessica Shaw
Editorial Intern: Alex Jacobs
Researchers: Ben Cameron, Cameron Hewitt, Helen Inman, Suzanne Kotz, Marijan Kriskovic, Cary Walker, Ian Watson
Maps & Graphics: David C. Hoerlein, Lauren Mills, Dawn Tessman Visser, Laura VanDeventer

Avalon Travel

Senior Editor and Series Manager: Madhu Prasher
Editor: Jamie Andrade
Associate Editor: Annette Kohl
Assistant Editor: Maggie Ryan
Copy Editor: Jennifer Malnick
Proofreader: Suzie Nasol
Indexer: Stephen Callahan
Cover Design: Kimberly Glyder Design
Maps & Graphics: Kat Bennett, Mike Morgenfeld

Title Page Photo: Piazza del Plebiscito, Naples, Italy © edella/www.123rf.com
Front Cover Photo: Cliffside Village, Amalfi Coast, Italy © Adeliepenguin/Dreamstime.com
Additional Photography: Dominic Bonuccelli, Ben Cameron, Jennifer Hauseman, Cameron Hewitt, David C. Hoerlein, Anne Jenkins, Gene Openshaw, Michael Potter, Robyn Stencil, Rick Steves, Bruce VanDeventer, Laura VanDeventer, Les Wahlstrom, Ian Watson, Wikimedia Commons

Although the author and publisher have made every effort to provide accurate, up-to-date information, they accept no responsibility for loss, injury, bad pasta, or inconvenience sustained by any person using this book.

ABOUT THE AUTHOR

RICK STEVES

 Since 1973, Rick Steves has spent 100 days every year exploring Europe. Along with writing and researching a bestselling series of guidebooks, Rick produces a public television series *(Rick Steves' Europe)*, a public radio show *(Travel with Rick Steves)*, and an app and podcast *(Rick Steves Audio Europe)*; writes a nationally syndicated newspaper column; organizes guided tours that take over ten thousand travelers to Europe annually; and offers an information-packed website (www.ricksteves.com). With the help of his hardworking staff of 80 at Europe Through the Back Door—in Edmonds, Washington, just north of Seattle—Rick's mission is to make European travel fun, affordable, and culturally enlightening for Americans.

Connect with Rick:

facebook.com/RickSteves   twitter: @RickSteves

Want More Italy?
Maximize the experience with Rick Steves as your guide

Guidebooks
Venice, Florence, and Rome guides make side-trips smooth and affordab

Phrase Books
Rely on Rick's Italian Phrase Book and Dictionary

Rick's DVDs
Preview where you're going with 15 shows on Italy

Free! Rick's Audio Europe™ App
Get free audio tours for Italy's top sights

Small-Group Tours
Rick offers a dozen great itineraries through Italy

For all the details, visit ricksteves.com